Become

Totally

Debt-Free

in

Five Years

or Less

*Pay off your mortgage, car,
credit cards and more!*

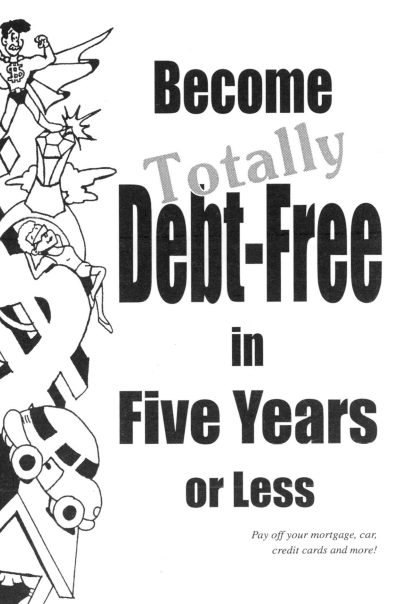

Gwendolyn D. Gabriel

self-proclaimed cheapskate ✳

BECOME TOTALLY DEBT-FREE

IN
FIVE YEARS
OR LESS

Pay off your mortgage, car, credit cards and more!

❖ ❖ ❖

by
Self-Proclaimed Cheapskate
Gwendolyn D. Gabriel

— First Edition —

Brown Bag Press, Dallas, Texas

First Printing

Book design: Stacy Luecker *(essex@fastlane.net)*
Illustrations: Raphael Elizalde
Editors: Chandra Sparks Taylor, Diana Kennedy

Published by BROWN BAG PRESS
P.O. Box 764585
Dallas, Texas 75376
1-877-522-4040

Includes bibliographical references and index.
Preassigned LCCN: 00-105826
ISBN: 0-9703022-0-7
Printed in the United States of America

Publisher's Cataloging-in-Publication

Gabriel, Gwendolyn D.
  Become totally debt-free in five years or less : pay off your mortgage, car, credit cards and more! / by Gwendolyn D. Gabriel ; [editors, Chandra Sparks Taylor, Diana Kennedy ; illustrations, Raphael Elizalde]. -- 1st ed.
  p. cm.
  Includes bibliographical references and index.
  LCCN: 00-105826
  ISBN: 0-9703022-0-7

  1. Finance, Personal. 2. Debt. I. Title.

HG179.G33 2000   332.024
                        QBI00-743

•••

    This book was written as a self-help guide for those who want or need to save money and become totally debt-free and, as such, provides much thought-provoking information in a number of areas. It is not the purpose of this book to provide all of the material available in each of these areas, but to package the information in a manner that is both enlightening and informative. Although the material in this book has been carefully researched and verified, there is the possibility that content and typographical errors exist. Also, the information is current only up to the date of publication.
    Further, it is not possible to provide information that is effective for everyone and in every geographical region. If, in reading this book, you require the services of an expert in any subject-matter or geographical area, then seek advice from competent professionals. Also, some of the ideas in this book may not be effective for everyone. Thus, you are encouraged to explore all available resources, especially the free or low-cost ones, in deciding how you will improve your financial condition.
    Having said this, the author and publisher do not accept any liability or responsibility for loss or damage, real or implied, which may be represented as a result of reading and implementing the techniques and ideas described in this book. *If you cannot accept and be bound by this disclaimer, please return this book in the condition in which it was purchased to receive a full refund.*

To my Lord and Savior,
who makes all things possible.

•••

To my mother: every moment spent in
your presence is
an honor.

•••

To my little ones, who will never know
how much they inspired me
to write this book.

About The Author

Gwendolyn D. Gabriel, a self-proclaimed cheapskate, is also an attorney and a real-estate broker. Of these titles, the thirty-three-year-old native Texan believes "cheapskate" is the one that has had the greatest impact on her life. Gabriel became totally debt-free in five years, by paying off all her debts, including her thirty-year mortgage loan. Being a cheapskate comes as naturally to Gabriel, as eating, breathing and sleeping. But she realizes that it may not come as natural to others, so she wrote this book to help others get out of debt too.

Gabriel earned a bachelor's degree in business administration from The University of Texas at Austin in 1987, a law degree from Southern Methodist University in Dallas in 1990 and received her real estate training at Cedar Valley College in Lancaster, Texas in 1994. Gabriel is married and this is her first literary work.

ACKNOWLEDGMENTS

I wish to thank my mother, who knew the importance of teaching me money-management skills, a valuable, life-long lesson on a subject that was not, and still is not taught in the more formal educational settings. Daddy, thank you, too, because you inadvertently taught me how I didn't want to manage my money. But, you know I love you.

I also wish to thank all of the friends and family members who shared stories of your financial woes with me. If it had not been for some of the personal experiences you contributed, then I might not have realized the need for this book. I won't call any names, Gina. (You are my sister girl and I love you dearly, but you and I both know that you need to be the first one in line to buy my book and follow every ounce of the advice that's in it.)

To my editors Chandra Sparks Taylor and Diana Kennedy, my graphic designer Stacy Luecker, my illustrator Raphael Elizalde, my Web site designer Roxanne Holt, and my husband Rick who read the entire manuscript more times than I can count, I sincerely thank you. In addition, thanks to the following authors: Michael Baisden, Victor McGlothin, Joann Tolbert-Yancy, Tammy (Nia) Atkins, Art Heine and Erle Rawlins III, for all the support, information and assistance you provided me as a new kid on the block.

Last, but not least, I wish to thank those who invested a little more than the cost of two regular-admission movie-theater tickets to buy my book. You won't regret you did, because you've just made a big investment in your financial future.

Basically, thanks to everyone, and that should just about do it because, if I continue, I'm going to start sounding like one of those long, drawn-out Academy Award acceptance speeches. All kidding aside, thanks to all who made this book possible and all who realize your possibilities of becoming debt-free by reading this book.

Introduction

I have written this self-help book on a common topic everyone needs to know about—saving money. Having given advice to others about saving money for so many years, I decided to write a book about this most sought-after topic. When I started telling people that I was writing a financial book, they'd respond, "Oh, I really need to read it."

Anyone who wants or needs to save money and become totally debt-free, but may not know how to do so, will benefit from this book. Whoever coined the phrase, "what you don't know won't hurt you," was wrong. I give several money-saving ideas that I didn't know about when I needed to, and not knowing ended up costing me thousands of dollars. (Read Sections 10:15 and 10:17.) So, I know firsthand, that not knowing can be detrimental to your financial condition.

This book is not just any old ordinary book about saving money and it's not written by just any ordinary author. It's about saving money to become totally debt-free. As you will read, I went from being $125,000 in debt (including credit-card debt, a car loan and a thirty-year mortgage) in 1994, to becoming totally debt-free by 1999. To help you accomplish the same, motivational messages as well as some money-saving ideas are included.

Most financial books that I've read are either too complicated to understand because they were written by financial planners/advisors, or they offer ridiculous, unrealistic or cumbersome ways to save (e.g., from buy a cow to get free milk or grow a garden to save money on vegetables, to marry a millionaire or don't have kids because they are expensive). This book is neither, because it is written by me, a self-proclaimed cheapskate who provides all of the simple, common-sense and creative techniques that I implemented, and that anyone can implement, to save money and become totally debt-free.

In addition to my techniques, please note that there are some money-saving ideas included that I haven't personally had to implement in order to become totally debt-free because they were not relevant to my financial situation. For example, although I've never had to file bankruptcy, I realize that some readers may be experiencing this, so I've included a section about filing for bankruptcy. Also, with regard to getting a traffic citation, my experience is from a prosecutor's perspective, not from the defendant's, and thus I provide my take on how you can increase your chances of not having to pay a traffic citation, as a former prosecutor.

In essence, I am very in tune with saving money so, in addition to providing you all of the ideas I implemented, I have used other sources to find additional ways to save money. By including these ideas, I hope the reader is better informed.

This book is also a source of motivation. Many books about saving money include the techniques you need to implement without the motivational messages to encourage you to implement them, or they include the motivational messages without providing you the techniques. This book provides you both, because you need both to successfully save money and become totally debt-free.

By implementing these ideas, you will be able to accumulate more money and assets than you've ever had before. It is my hope that you will enjoy reading my book as much as I've enjoyed writing it, and that you will enjoy your savings and debt-free status even more!

—**Gwendolyn D. Gabriel**

CONTENTS

Chapter 18 — Clothes, Shoes, Jewelry, Etc.

Chapter 19 — Career

Chapter 20 — Transportation

Chapter 24 — Because It Makes Sense

Chapter 25 — Entertainment

BECOME
TOTALLY
DEBT-FREE
IN
FIVE YEARS
OR LESS

Overview

Before telling you about myself and my qualifications to write this book, I will tell you about one of my biggest accomplishments, which is the reason why I wrote this book. I became totally debt-free, including paying off my thirty-year mortgage loan, in five years.

Approximately five years ago, I barely qualified to purchase the $96,000 four-bedroom, two-and-a-half-bath home with a two-car garage, swimming pool and other amenities I now own free and clear. My salary at the time was about $38,000 a year—a bit more than a modest salary to go along with a little more than modest 2,200-square-foot home.

When I first purchased my home, I was paying about $850 a month (principal, interest, taxes and insurance) on a thirty-year mortgage loan and not really looking forward to paying this amount over the next thirty years. During this time, I also had a $450 monthly car note, for which I still owed about $20,000. I had more than $5,000 in credit-card debt and $5,000 in my savings. I was netting about $1,900 a month and my total monthly expenses were about $1,700 a month. I saw no way out of debt and knew I wasn't content with working just to be able to pay my monthly bills, which included my mortgage, for the next thirty years. I had to do something. So, I used the techniques described here to save money and eventually pay off some of my debts.

Little did I know that five years later, I would save enough money to pay off my credit-card debt, my car loan and my mortgage loan, in that order. I have to admit I didn't plan this initially, but as I began to see how much I was really able to save, I started believing I could do it—and I did it! I'm so happy about my accomplishments that I'm eager to tell everyone how I did it and the impact it has already had on my life after only a few months.

Specifically, I went from saving $200 a month in 1994, to saving $4,000 a month in 1999. The home I qualified to purchase on a thirty-year term in 1994, soon became a home I would eventually pay off in 1999. The premise: If I was able to qualify for a certain mortgage amount, then I earned enough to pay off my mortgage loan in five years if I were to incorporate some money-saving ideas. The same premise holds true for you.

You may think it makes sense to pay off a car loan, credit-card debts and any other non-tax–deductible debts expeditiously. But, you may wonder why someone would want to pay off their mortgage loan when they benefit by deducting the interest paid when filing their income taxes each year. Well, I consulted with a tax accountant and we reviewed exactly how much I would benefit by having this deduction versus not having the deduction if I paid off my house. We determined that any way you look at it, paying off a mortgage loan and not having a house note is the most beneficial way to live for several reasons:

First, not having a house note allows you more financial and career flexibility. You are not financially strapped with paying what most people would consider their biggest monthly debt.

Second, during the first ten years of a thirty-year mortgage, only 5% to 10% of your monthly mortgage note goes toward your principal loan balance, while sometimes more than 50% goes toward your mortgage interest (the cost you pay to borrow the money). The remaining percentage accounts for your property taxes, property insurance, mortgage insurance (if your down payment is less than 20%), and escrow shortages.

Third, your tax benefit by deducting the mortgage interest paid is minimal when compared to the amount of money you would save by paying off your mortgage loan early. In other words, maintaining a mortgage note just to be able to deduct your mortgage interest payments is less beneficial to you than paying off your mortgage note and not having this deduction. (Note: A further explanation of the benefits of paying off your mortgage loan is given in Section 11:1.) Besides, there are other deductions for which you may qualify, such as property taxes, which you can't avoid; or church contributions, which may bring you joy; or job related expenses, which may be tied to your income. (See Section 29:1 for more deductions.)

Fourth, if you paid off your mortgage loan, you could then save 100% of the money that you would have ordinarily applied toward your loan, including mortgage interest charges, and apply it toward your retirement. Or, you could pay off your mortgage loan and, as discussed in Section 24:14, invest the money. By doing this, and with good investments, you could make more money from your investments and save more in mortgage interest charges than if you just paid your monthly mortgage payment over the next thirty years and applied any extra money toward your investments.

Ultimately, by paying off your mortgage loan, you will have tackled the biggest obstacle toward becoming totally debt-free, and you will have increased your flexibility to do whatever you choose with the excess money. In essence, you will have gained financial freedom.

So, what does being debt-free or having financial freedom really mean? Of course it doesn't mean you are able to live and not have to use any money or pay for anything. There are just some things even a debt-free person cannot escape, such as property taxes (which are tax deductible), property insurance, utilities, car/household repairs and the bare necessities of living—food and clothing. As you can see, being debt-free doesn't mean you don't have to have money.

What being debt-free does mean is you have the flexibility to not be tied to a stress-filled job that provides your main or only source of income. Specifically, being debt-free may provide you the opportunity to retire early; take a break from working altogether; spend less time working and more time with your family; spend more time doing what you enjoy; move from a high-stressed, better-paying job to a less-stressed environment; quit your job to start your own business; work part-time instead of full-time; become a stay-at-home parent; go from a two-income to a one-income family and so on. The common denominator to all of the above is the flexibility you would gain in order to exercise any of these options if you were to become debt-free.

However, your flexibility and the time you are able to exercise these options depend on a couple of factors: how much money you have accumulated as a debt-free person to pay for bare essentials, and whether you have another source of income and another means of health coverage. Overall, being able to exercise your options, even with some limitations, can make you very happy.

While it is true that money can't buy you happiness, having financial freedom can give you options and some sense of control over your own happiness. For me, only a month after becoming debt-free, I began to see my options and, for the first time, I felt in total control of my life. The bottom line is that being debt-free means you have the flexibility of not being strapped in a high-stressed job or an unhappy situation with very few options.

Now, a little bit about myself and my qualifications to write this book: I'm in my early thirties. I was born and raised in Dallas, Texas, and I still continue to live in the Dallas area, along with all of my immediate family members and most of my relatives. (You will find I give Texas as an example for several of the money-saving tips presented in my book.)

I married three years ago, and my husband and I believed it was, and still is, in our best interest to maintain separate financial situations. Specifically, in anticipation of writing this book, at the time we married, I was well on my way to accomplishing my goals of paying off my mortgage loan and becoming totally debt-free. Thus, I knew if I was to accomplish this goal and let others know what I did and how I did it, I didn't want help from anyone. I wanted to be able to honestly say I did it all by myself.

I am an attorney who, after eight years of working for one employer, earns a modest salary. I became a real-estate broker three years ago. At the time I purchased my home, I knew very little about qualifying for a mortgage loan, purchasing a home, mortgage interest rates and points, what a mortgage note consisted of, etc. To better prepare you for the home-buying experience, I provide a chapter on this subject.

Besides being an attorney and a real-estate broker, I am a self-proclaimed cheapskate, and have been ever since I first learned to count money. Being a cheapskate comes naturally to me. I realize that for some people, it doesn't come as naturally and may have to be learned. However, learning to become a cheapskate may be the single, most valuable lesson that will undoubtedly have a positive impact on the rest of your life. Having spent seven years in college and law school combined, I still believe my money-management knowledge is the most valuable to me.

This leads me to the point of why I decided to write this book. The reason is twofold. First, I want to tell people of my personal accomplishment of going from being $125,000 in debt to becoming totally debt-free in five years. Then, I want to encourage and motivate others by letting you know that you, too, can achieve financial success. You may ask, what is financial success? It is not being one of the world's richest people, having more material possessions, wearing the best clothes, driving the fanciest car, etc. Financial success is being happy about your individual financial situation, not having to worry about where you are going to get the money to pay your bills and, in essence, it means being debt-free.

Approximately 98% of the people I know are in some sort of financial trouble, which is causing them much stress in their lives. In fact, these people are far from becoming debt-free. I don't like seeing people, especially those dear to me, repeating financial mistakes that usually last a lifetime. So, while I was working toward becoming debt-free, I attempted to motivate others by letting them know how and why I was saving money.

Little did I know that I would be faced with much opposition when I attempted to do so. Over the last few years, it wasn't easy telling others about how I was implementing my money-saving techniques because they teased me about my frugality. It seems as if the more I attempted to convince others that saving, not spending, is the way to go, the more they teased me. Sometimes at parties or dinners, the intricate details of my frugality would be the focus of the conversation and laughter. Hearing others make fun of my frugality began to make me laugh harder than anyone else, and I'd ask myself, *Do others really see me that way?* The answer, yes they do; only now, as a debt-free person, they want to be just like me.

It was at the point when I told others I had paid off my mortgage loan, car loan and credit-card debts, and had become totally debt-free, that they knew they wanted to do the same thing. They stopped laughing and started listening.

When I talked to others one on one, in defense of their own perceived financial inadequacies, they responded in one of several ways: "Why save, you can't take it with you when you die?" My response: "No you can't take it with you, but being debt-free sure does buy you a lot of peace of mind and flexibility regarding your life and financial situation while you are alive."

Second: "I work hard every day to earn my money, so I'm going to enjoy the fruits of my labor" or "spending the paycheck I work hard for, makes me happy." My response: "Saving your money toward financial freedom is enjoying the fruits of your labor, and thereby would make you happier." Despite this response, many people believe that I am not really enjoying the fruits of my labor and thus, I am not a happy person because I save and carefully spend my money, or because my hobbies don't include activities that involve spending money—shopping and more shopping.

Most people I know view shopping and spending as their keys to happiness. These activities come more naturally to them than saving. For most of these people, they will continue a lifetime of indebtedness, failing to take control over their own financial situations. This is not a good way to live for anyone and it may result in a lot of unhappiness.

Even while saving and accomplishing all of my financial goals, I enjoy more than the average number of annual trips for what it might cost a non-frugal vacationer to take one trip. I can find ten or more great wardrobe items for the cost of what a non-frugal shopper may pay for one or two comparable outfits. I feel I have more fun on a daily basis spending time with my family and friends and participating in free activities, like playing cards and dominos or talking with family members, than a shopper/spender. In actuality, shopping or spending money doesn't make me happy one bit. The bottom line: As a cheapskate, I believe I have everything I want and need and have more fun than most non-frugal people I know, with the difference being I also enjoy the financial freedom to exercise my options, while they remain financially strapped.

Now that I am debt-free, I plan to quit my job within the next couple of years. I would also like to practice a little law and maybe a little real estate on the side. In addition, I'm looking forward to spending more time with my family and living a low-stress or no-stress life.

Back to the responses I've received when I talked to others about the importance of saving money and becoming debt-free. Another response was, "I don't make enough money to do what you are doing," or "I have more bills and expenses than you." My response: "There is no good excuse."

I believe that how much you earn is not as important as what you do with what you earn. I know many people who earn more than others, yet they are worse off financially than those who earn less. So, it doesn't matter how little or how much you earn. You just have to know what to do and have the motivation and discipline to do it.

I realize that each of you, in beginning this endeavor to become totally debt-free, will be starting at different points. It would be extremely unlikely and highly coincidental to start out exactly where I started out both financially and emotionally. Your debt or income may differ from mine, as I'm sure other aspects of your financial history will. But, from a financial aspect, it doesn't matter where you are starting, as much as the realization that you need to start, the mind frame under which you will start and the motivation and discipline you possess to continue the process all the way to the end.

To approach your goal of becoming totally debt-free in less than five years, read this book from the beginning to get a feel for how you will change and improve your lifestyle regarding saving and spending money. In addition, complete all of the exercises and worksheets and review at least one or two of the ideas that are in this book every day. Determine which ideas will work best for you, then gradually begin to implement them until you have the optimum combination of ideas that work for you.

In conjunction with making this book a part of your everyday reading, assess whether this book alone is enough for you to improve your ideas and attitude regarding saving and spending money. Some people seek psychological counseling to overcome depression, stop smoking, decrease their stress level, improve a bad marriage or to overcome a traumatic life experience. Why wouldn't you be open to the idea of individual counseling or group therapy to improve the way in which you handle money?

While reading this book, evaluate whether individual or group counseling will be beneficial to help you overcome money-management problems. It is my opinion that the more resources you seek, the greater the likelihood that you will improve your financial condition toward becoming debt-free. That's the goal I want you to achieve in reading this book.

This book is divided into four parts: the overview, "Getting the Right Mind-set," "Now It's Time to Become Debt-Free," and the finale. The next part, entitled "Getting the Right Mind-set," includes information on understanding how you became the financial being you are, a couple of self-evaluations and inspirational and motivational messages to get you in the right frame of mind to get started. The third part, entitled "Now It's Time to Become Debt-Free," provides all of the techniques I implemented and then some, based on my own and other's personal experiences regarding saving and spending. The finale provides you additional motivation to keep you on the right track to saving money and includes some worksheets you should implement to ensure you save money successfully and become totally debt-free.

In addition, at the end of each chapter, I provide you with an affirmation. The next time you pull out a dollar bill, before you spend it, repeat one of these affirmations.

While implementing the ideas in this book, I challenge you to use your creativity to find some money-saving techniques of your own. You may come up with techniques that work for you; or, you may use a combination of some of the techniques in my book and ones you create.

Whatever you use, the most important thing is that you get started now! This book provides you the solid foundation you need to start and continue the process all the way to the end. Each topic is presented like I like it—short, simple and to the point—without boring you with a lot of unnecessary details. Remember, I became debt-free by using these techniques and ideas, so can you!

Yours Truly,

Gwendolyn Gabriel
The Cheapskate

PART I

GETTING the RIGHT MIND-SET

CHAPTER 1

From Whence We Came

1:1   Analyzing Our Financial Decisions

Why do we make the financial decisions we do? Some of us have developed attitudes and behaviors toward money from our parents or others who influenced our lives. We grew up seeing how our parents handled money and we ended up subconsciously handling money the way we saw them do it for years, whether good or bad. Then, there are others who grew up either extremely rich or extremely poor and this often has an effect, mostly a negative one, on the way we handle money throughout our lives. There could be many familial, environmental or psychological factors as to why each of us handles money the way we do. Sometimes there is no logical reason or factor to justify our handling of money.

For me, I believe I was influenced by my mother. I grew up in a two-parent, middle-class home with a brother and a sister. My father loved to spend money and my mother loved to budget and save. My sister, even today, will admit she has a serious money-management problem, while my brother and I are extremely frugal. I'm more frugal than my mother, and my sister, I believe, is even more of a spend-thrift than my father. So, maybe individually, each of our parents had an effect on how my sister, my brother and I, as adults, handle money.

I think it is important for you to understand what or who may have influenced your attitudes and behaviors toward money because it helps you better understand yourself. It's even more important for you to realize that you will be better off if you improve your financial situation. I'm not saying you have to become as frugal as I am, or that if you do, you will be happy. I am saying that if you improve your attitudes and behaviors toward money, then you are better prepared to become totally debt-free. By doing this, you've just bought yourself some peace of mind regarding your individual financial situation. A person who has this peace of mind is generally a person who is happier.

1:2   Why Some Adults Can't Manage Money

There may be several reasons why adults have money-management problems. The lack of knowledge on how to deal with these problems can be one of the biggest causes of why so many families, generation after generation, continue to suffer financially. But, with regard to your lack of knowledge in dealing with money-management issues, it may not be totally your fault.

Remember back in high school when you were learning calculus, art and science? There wasn't a class in money management. Unless you are in the calculus, art or science field, how many times do you need those subjects to make it from day to day? Probably none. So, it really isn't your fault that you were never formally taught how to manage your money effectively. How did you learn to effectively manage money? You either had to teach yourself, or you inadvertently learned from your parents (whether their ways of managing money were good or bad), or you just never really learned.

What if schools had a money-management requirement? These courses wouldn't necessarily have to teach students how to be frugal, but simply how to manage their money effectively. Perhaps the courses could include a semester-long project with the curriculum entailing detailed money-management scenarios and problem-solving techniques. How well the student does in the course would depend on how effective he became at handling his finances. This type of course could prove to be the lesson of a lifetime.

Getting back to real life. If you have children, then understand that they are less likely to take these types of courses in financial responsibility within the school environment we have today because most schools don't offer them. But, you can make sure your children learn this information, in addition to other subjects, at home. There is only one catch—you have to develop a solid grasp on effective lifelong, money-management techniques yourself and put them into practice before you can effectively teach your children—or others. If more people were to learn how to manage their money effectively and teach their children to do the same, this country would have a lot less bankruptcies, and a lot more financially stable families—generation after generation.

1:3   Learning from Past Mistakes

I do have some regrets about how I have made use of my money. If you have never had regrets regarding any of your past decisions handling money, then you are a rarity. Not too many people can say that. Just because some of us have made mistakes in the past, doesn't mean we have to continue making them.

I'm sure you know of people who have made some financial mistakes that you haven't. You have probably made some that they haven't. Because money-management mistakes come in so many different forms, once you've made one, doesn't mean you have learned your lesson and will never make another.

Here are some suggestions on how to minimize the number of money-management mistakes you make in the future. First, learn from your own, as well as others' mistakes. Second, don't repeat a mistake—yours or someone else's. Third, learn not only from your errors, but from past successes you and others have had with money. Finally, when you've made a good decision regarding money, cherish it and share it with someone else.

I refuse to live without money, so I won't.

CHAPTER 2

Take a Look at Yourself

2:1   Money Psychological Evaluation

Take this short money psychological evaluation to determine how you view your own money-management situation. After each of the five phrases, circle the column (A or B), with the two responses that best describe your attitude regarding money. If neither column fits how you would respond or if only one response in a column fits, then choose the column, which provides the responses that are closest to your attitude, and please be honest with yourself.

1. I would save more money if...

Column A	Column B
...I had a better paying job.	...I budgeted more wisely.
...I didn't have so many bills.	...I didn't spend so much money on things I wanted.

2. I would have fewer debts if...

Column A	Column B
...I didn't have to pay so many bills.	...I would stop charging on my credit cards.
...I didn't have to pay so much on things I need, e.g., rent and food.	...I didn't shop or spend unnecessarily.

3. I need more money because...

Column A	Column B
...I need or want to buy so many things.	...I do unnecessary shopping or spending.
...I don't have enough money left over after I pay all of my bills.	...I buy things I really don't need.

4. I spend a lot of money because...

Column A	Column B
...I enjoy buying things I like.	...I buy things I really don't need.
...shopping makes me feel happy or less depressed.	...I may have a shopping or spending problem.

5. It's hard to make ends meet because...

Column A	Column B
...I have too many bills to pay.	...I don't budget my money wisely.
...I don't make enough money.	...I don't spend my money wisely.

Number in Column A circled: _____

Number in Column B circled: _____

Once you have completed this money psychological evaluation, determine whether your responses were more like the ones in column A or column B above. Did you circle more column A's or more column B's? If you circled more column A's, then you are blaming someone else or something else for your money-management problems. If you circled more column B's, then you have appropriately taken full responsibility for your own money-management problems. So, now what do you do?

It is important to first realize that you and only you are in control of your money-management situation. Blaming someone or something else for your money-management problems won't do you any good as you begin to solve these problems. Begin by blaming *only* yourself. By accepting full responsibility, you have just taken the first step toward repairing your financial problems and becoming totally debt-free. The next step is to take the necessary actions to repair your money-management problems.

2:2   The Ultimate Test

		True	False
1.	You enjoy shopping as a pastime.	✓	
2.	In the past two months, you've purchased clothing or a pair of shoes for yourself.	✓	
3.	You sometimes buy things you don't need just because they're on sale.	✓	
4.	You sometimes shop either when you are really depressed or in a really great mood.	✓	
5.	You prefer buying brand names and designer labels.		✓
6.	You have more than one credit card.		✓
7.	You purchase or would like to purchase a car at least once every three to five years.		✓
8.	You believe that if you had more money, you wouldn't have financial problems.		✓

	True	**False**
9. If you lost your main source of income today you wouldn't have enough money to make ends meet for the next six months.	✓	
10. You've had to borrow money from someone you know in the last year.		✓
11. You believe that it would be hard to save money because you have a lot of bills and debts.	✓	
12. You believe that the more you pay for a product, the better it is.		✓

This is really a test to determine whether or not you are a cheapskate. With many people suffering from financial ruin these days, being considered a cheapskate is (or it should be anyway) an honor. The closer you are to being considered a cheapskate, the easier it may be for you to adapt to, and implement the ideas in this book.

On the contrary, the further you are from being considered a cheapskate, the harder it may be for you to adapt. No matter how far you are from being considered a cheapskate, it is not impossible, and definitely not too late, for you to become one. So, let's determine how you did.

Tally up your number of "true" responses. Then, read the synopsis below to see where you are on the cheapskate scale.

Number of "true" responses: 6

How did you do?

0–2   You are a true cheapskate. Keep up the good work!

3–5   You are not considered a cheapskate yet. But you are close to becoming one. Keep doing what you're doing and improve upon that.

6–8   No doubt you have some major problems managing your money. But you realize you can do better. Now, it's up to you to just do it.

9–12   You spend money like it's water. If you are not there already, then you are headed for financial ruin. Stop the spending and start saving now.

When I look in the mirror,
I see financial stability—
I see myself.

CHAPTER 3

Improve Your Financial Outlook

3:1   The First Step to Recovery Is Admission

If you have a problem managing money, you must first admit it. You don't have to be honest with anyone but yourself. If you remain in denial, then you will not improve, and you will continue to have problems managing money.

3:2   Living Beyond Your Means?

If after you pay all of your bills and other necessary expenses, you don't have at least 20% of your net income left over, then you are probably living beyond your means. Although you may not be able to change the fact that you have to pay rent/mortgage or a car note right now, there are ways to decrease your other expenses. Such changes could include implementing ways to cut your utility expenses in half, making the most of your wardrobe without buying more clothes and cutting back on your eating expenses.

Some ways to decrease your monthly expenses are within your control and are things you can and should implement immediately. Some are not, which is understandable, so change the things you can now and develop a plan as to how you will eventually decrease or eliminate your less flexible expenses. Your goal should be to adjust your lifestyle so you can live as close to your means as possible.

3:3   Please Don't Try to Keep Up

Most people love competition. However, competition is not always good. I'm sure you've heard of the phrase "trying to keep up with the Joneses." But, it can't hurt to reiterate that you shouldn't try to keep up with your neighbors or friends, whether they are the Joneses, the Smiths or the Jacksons.

Trying to acquire material possessions because others have them is a financial no-no. You don't know the financial position of the Joneses, or what they could be doing to acquire the things they have, so it doesn't make sense to try to keep up with them. Even if you do know the Joneses' financial situation, you still shouldn't try to have what they have just because they have it. Doing so could land you in a financial situation that may not be good for you.

If you are a natural competitor, try competing with anyone who will accept the challenge to save the most money and become totally debt-free within the shortest amount of time. Under this circumstance, by all means, please do try to keep up.

3:4   Don't Try to Impress

Trying to dazzle others by buying expensive cars or clothing can land you in deep financial trouble; meanwhile, those who you are trying to impress could be robbing Peter to pay Paul, just to impress you. Besides, what benefit is it to you for others to consider you the best dressed, to compliment you on the type of car you drive or to be awed by the amount of money you are able to spend on material possessions?

Associate yourself with people who you don't feel a need to have to impress. Or, if you feel you must amaze others, associate with people who are more excited by your motivation to save money and accomplish your financial goals than the type of car you drive. These people will be even more overwhelmed when you tell them you have become totally debt-free. Also, whether or not they admit it, those who end up in financial trouble by trying to impress you, will also be fascinated if you tell them you've become debt-free.

3:5   Share Money-Saving Ideas with Others

Tell anyone and everyone who will listen about your newfound financial goals toward becoming totally debt-free. Continue to talk about the subject. The more you talk about your financial goals, the more they will stay on your mind, which is just what you need to say no to unnecessary spending.

In addition to telling others about your financial goals, ask them if they have any additional suggestions or ideas of ways you can save. They may even start thinking about creating some goals of their own. Just as you have started on the right track, you may be the motivation others need to get started.

3:6   You Can Benefit from a Support Group

Join or start a support group that includes others who are in debt, but are on the journey to becoming debt-free. Support groups have proven to be successful because, if you think about it, there are so many that cover issues people deal with on a daily basis, or are faced with at some point in their lives. There are few, if any, that deal with improving money management. However, the lack of availability or existence of such support groups is not evidence that money management is not a serious problem.

If you feel you would benefit from joining a support group, but don't know of any to join, start one. Create your own rules, e.g., how often you will meet, what financial topics you will discuss and where you will meet. Make sure if you start a support group, you give 100% of your efforts so that others will want to join, continue to come to the group meetings and feel that they are benefiting from being part of the group. A support group can be an effective tool to improve your management of money.

3:7   Make This Book a Book Club Topic

Most book clubs select all sorts of material to discuss. For your next meeting, select this book. By doing so, you're discussing two topics everyone needs to know more about—saving money and becoming debt-free. I have a feeling that by reading and sharing ideas about these topics, the members are going to benefit.

CHAPTER 4

You Can Do It

4:1 Realize It's Never Too Late

Ever feel that your financial condition is beyond repair? That it's hopeless? You must realize that it will not improve overnight. It may only take one or two bad financial choices and a short period to negatively affect your financial condition; but, it takes a change in your attitude and behavior toward money, and months or even years to repair it. Don't get discouraged.

You must believe that no matter how hopeless you think your financial situation may be, there is hope. You have to believe that you can improve your condition and begin to do so, whether it means making some minor improvements or taking drastic measures such as filing for bankruptcy. But, realize it's never too late to start.

You are in control. You must decide when you are ready to make some changes and improvements regarding your own financial condition. You must understand that whether it's now or later, the decisions you make may affect the rest of your life. They may also affect your children and grandchildren's lives because you may be the main or only source of information they will have regarding managing money and making sound financial decisions. So you must make improvements, if not for yourself, for your future generations.

4:2   Changing Your Way of Life

If you are trying to lose weight, what do you do? You change your eating habits by reducing your intake of fat grams and calories, and you increase your amount of physical activity. Successfully losing weight and keeping it off requires a change in your lifestyle and frame of mind. Changing your financial position for the better is no different.

Once you get to the point where you believe that budgeting and saving are better than having on a new outfit or driving around in a new car, then you are on your way to improving your condition. Being financially stable and becoming debt-free will no doubt change your financial condition for the better.

4:3   Change Is Hard But Not Impossible

Old habits are hard to break, but they're not impossible. You must first realize that you need to improve your money-management habits, then you must want to change. Finally, you must believe that you can do it. If you believe in yourself, you are more likely to be successful in changing by improving your old money-management habits.

4:4   What's Luck Got to Do with It?

Absolutely nothing. Some people blame their unfortunate financial conditions on their bad luck. But, luck has nothing to do with whether you are living from paycheck to paycheck or whether you are financially stable.

Luck, whether good or bad, is something you have no control over, an accident. For example, a good break is buying a Powerball lottery ticket and hitting the eighty-million-dollar jackpot, when your chances of winning were only one in eighty million. A misfortune is being at a stadium, watching a football game in the rain along with fifty thousand other folks and being struck by lightning. Being in a bad financial situation or not being able to pay your bills is not something based on luck.

As discussed in the overview, you may not have control over a lot of things, but your financial situation is not one of them. So, don't blame a mishap for your bad financial condition. If you do, then you have succumbed to the belief that your financial condition has nothing to do with the choices and decisions you make, and that there is nothing you can do to improve it.

Start today believing that your financial situation has *everything* to do with your money-management decisions. Then, you can start making better financial decisions and stop blaming bad luck.

4:5   Prepare Yourself Mentally

To go from spending most of your money to saving most of it requires that you get mentally prepared. In fact, it is the key to successfully improving your money-management habits and ultimately becoming debt-free. To begin, you must first convince yourself that saving money is what you really want or need to do. Then, start repeating to yourself, "I can do this, I can do this." Next, you must start believing that you really can do it. Once you believe you can improve your financial condition and you want to improve it, then and only then are you mentally prepared to begin the journey to a debt-free life.

4:6   Discipline Yourself

Each of us has to have some sort of discipline in our lives, so why not set boundaries for yourself with regard to money? If you don't, you will end up having no control over your own financial situation. Some of you may already be there. Instead of continuing this lack of control, discipline yourself. When you do well, reward yourself. For instance, if you have set a goal not to go to the mall or buy clothes or shoes for six months and, at the end of that time, you have successfully completed your goal, then reward yourself by spending a small amount (e.g., five to ten dollars) on something you really want.

On the other hand, when you lack control, don't justify your misdeeds. If you end up going to the mall or buying clothes or shoes for yourself within the six-month period, don't justify your actions by saying, "I really did need this outfit" or "I really did need this pair of shoes." Instead, "punish" yourself for not keeping your goal by maybe extending the time you will be restricted.

To maintain control over your financial situation, you need to limit yourself. When doing so, be strict. But not too strict that you will be more apt to give up. With self-discipline, you are bound to succeed in improving your financial situation.

4:7   Enjoy Life as a Cheapskate

Being a cheapskate doesn't mean you can't enjoy life; it just means you enjoy life while making a conscious effort to budget and save money. If you admit you get pleasure from actually spending money, then I would suggest you first realize that this is a problem, especially if you don't have the money to do this. Even if you do have the money, unless you are a multimillionaire, spending for the sake of spending may be detrimental to your financial condition in the long run. Take the necessary steps to convince yourself that, as a cheapskate, you can enjoy life too.

4:8   Don't Be Ashamed, Be Frugal

When I was younger, I was teased and talked about because of my frugality. Those who know me would make statements such as, "You're so tight, your butt squeaks when you walk." My feelings would get hurt and I would be sad. Those days are long gone.

Today, when people joke about my frugality, I not only laugh with them, but I think to myself, *You are going to one day wish you were like me*. Being a cheapskate has allowed me to make financial accomplishments. Because of these accomplishments, specifically having become totally debt-free, I am truly proud to be considered a cheapskate, even though I have been teased about it all of my life.

Once you have begun to make a lifestyle change and have become a cheapskate, I feel it's your choice whether or not you want others to know how frugal you have become. With so many people having financial problems nowadays, don't be ashamed of becoming frugal. Instead, consider it a privilege, and an honor, to be called a cheapskate. I do.

4:9   Keep Your Eyes on the Prize

Whether your goal is to pay off your mortgage loan in less than five years and to become totally debt-free, or you have different financial goals, you must keep your eyes on the prize. Keep focused and make goals that are attainable. For example, if you save $10,000 a year, then an obtainable goal may be to pay off a $100,000 mortgage loan in about ten years, not five. If you save $20,000 a year, then you are able to pay off a $100,000 mortgage loan in five years, not two or three. So, make sure your goals are obtainable. Nothing is more discouraging than not meeting a goal you've set for yourself.

Maybe you have multiple goals. For instance, you may want to pay off your house and save toward your retirement and your children's college education, all at the same time. If you decide to do this, specify the total amount of money you will need to complete each goal. Then, allocate a certain amount of money each month into separate accounts. (The amount depends on the deadline you have and how much money you will need to complete each goal.)

PART II

Now It's Time to Become Debt-Free

CHAPTER 5

Improve Your Financial Condition

5:1   Are You a Candidate for Bankruptcy?

Bankruptcy gives a person the opportunity to relieve himself of debt through a federal proceeding. Filing bankruptcy, however, is not for everyone in debt. When considering whether you should file bankruptcy, it is important for you to determine if the benefits outweigh the consequences. It is also important to understand the two main types of consumer bankruptcy and which is best for you. In addition, understand that some debts—such as student loans, back taxes, debt owed to government entities and child-support and alimony payments and arrearages—are not dismissed by filing bankruptcy.

The two types of consumer bankruptcies are Chapter Seven and Chapter Thirteen. Chapter Seven is for people with a lot of unsecured debts, but with very few or no secured assets, e.g., they may have a car or a house with very little equity. It removes all of your unsecured debts, e.g., credit-card balances, medical bills and unsecured personal loans. (Note: A secured debt is one that is attached to real or personal property;

an unsecured debt is one not attached to any real or personal property.) Further, it is for those who have secured assets, e.g., a mortgage or a car, in which they are not behind on making the payments or can get caught up on the payments.

According to one Dallas bankruptcy attorney, if you are not behind or can get caught up paying on your secured assets based on your income and the amount of debt you're in, you have mostly unsecured debts, and you figure it would take you several years to pay off these debts, then you may want to consider filing Chapter Seven bankruptcy. This wipes away most of your unsecured debts, while allowing you to keep paying on your non-delinquent secured assets. In essence, it gives you a chance to start over. In addition, a Chapter Seven bankruptcy can usually be completed within a four- to six-month period.

On the other hand, Chapter Thirteen bankruptcy puts you on a three- to five-year repayment plan to pay as much of your debt, both secured and unsecured, as you can based on your disposable income. Thus, to file Chapter Thirteen bankruptcy, you must be earning some sort of income because it is more of a reorganization of your debt, which is not wiped away, as with Chapter Seven.

Your payments are made through a trustee's office that decides which creditors get paid, in what order and how much they will get, based on a statutory scheme. By making payments through a trustee, you are allowed to keep your secured assets as long as you keep up with your payments. Upon completion of the three- to five-year repayment plan, with the exception of a mortgage loan that you still must continue to pay on in order to maintain possession of the property, all of your remaining unsecured and some secured debts are wiped away.

This type of bankruptcy is for people whose delinquencies include mostly secured debt such as a mortgage or car loan, and they are behind in payments, but want to keep their assets. According to one bankruptcy attorney in Dallas, if you owe the IRS in back taxes, you are threatened with repossession and/or your house is about to go into foreclosure, then you may want to consider filing Chapter Thirteen, which may save you from losing your house and car, and it stops the penalties and interest from continuing to accrue on any back taxes owed to the IRS.

Some of the consequences of filing bankruptcy include: negative effects on your credit for up to ten years, which may affect your ability to obtain future credit, restrict your job options, and impede you from qualifying for a mortgage loan or limit the amount for which you qualify. If you don't file bankruptcy, as long as you have the debts that you are not paying on, your creditors may take legal action to foreclose on or repossess your secured assets; your creditors may harass you by calling you at work (with certain limitations), home and anywhere else they can find you; your creditors may also file lawsuits against you for your bad debts, and consequently obtain a judgment against you; and you would still have bad credit.

Factors such as your individual circumstances and the bankruptcy laws should be considered before filing bankruptcy. You must determine the amount of debt you're in and how long it would take you to pay off that debt if you do not file for bankruptcy.

While reviewing your financial circumstances, ask yourself the following questions: Are you falling further and further behind in your bills? If you applied every penny you had after paying your necessary living expenses toward your unsecured debts (e.g., credit cards) for the next several years, will you still not have paid off all of your unsecured debts? Is your financial situation totally hopeless? Are your creditors harassing you? Are your creditors unwilling to work with you to repay your debts, e.g., to reduce the balances owed, your interest rates or remove late fees and over-the-limit charges? (Note: In order not to incur more debt, you should try to work with your creditors yourself, instead of paying a company to negotiate for you.) If you answered yes to any of the aforementioned questions, then you should probably consider filing bankruptcy.

If you are uncertain whether you should file bankruptcy, schedule a consultation with an attorney who handles bankruptcy cases before making your decision. The attorney should be able to spell out the legalities for you, but the decision should be yours to make. Given some additional research, you can even file your own bankruptcy without hiring an attorney and save yourself hundreds of dollars in legal fees, although you'd still have to pay the bankruptcy filing fees. Purchasing one of those do-it-yourself kits or finding books that instruct you on how to file your own bankruptcy should also assist you.

5:2 Do a Periodic Checkup

Just as important as your annual health checkup, is a financial checkup. You can do your own financial checkup by listing your total monthly income, e.g., salary, and your total monthly expenses, e.g., mortgage/rent and food. Then, subtract your expenses from your income. This gives you the amount of your monthly disposable income. (Complete "Your Periodic Checkup," below.)

Whatever your disposable income, you should be saving or investing most of that amount. If you can't do so now, start off by saving 75% of your total monthly disposable income or 20% of your total monthly net income (your income after all taxes and other payroll deductions), whichever is greater. Then, month by month, increase this percentage. Once you start implementing the ideas in this book, you should have a higher disposable income of which to save, so that you will eventually accumulate enough money to pay off, one by one, all of your debts.

Your Periodic Checkup

Monthly Income

Monthly Net Income   _10,459_

Other Monthly Income   _____
(e.g., home-based business income,
child support and rental income)

                          Total Monthly Income _10,459_

Monthly Expenses

Mortgage/Rent   _12,339_

Car/Transportation/Gasoline   _2070_

Utilities   _500_
(e.g., electricity, water, gas and telephone)

Car Insurance   _243_

Health Insurance/Medical Expenses   _30_

Life Insurance   _____

Child Care	-0-
Food/Grocery Bills	300
Clothing/Shoes	100
Other *(e.g. credit cards)*	4,000

Total Monthly Expenses 9582

Monthly Income – Monthly Expenses = Monthly Disposable Income

Your Total Monthly Disposable Income = 877

5:3 Establish a Budget and Stick to It

Most people I know can't tell you where their paychecks go each month. All they know is that they don't have enough money to make ends meet. That's like having a checking account, writing checks, and never balancing it. Don't leave the management of your money to chance like that. Establish a budget and stick to it. However, before you can establish a budget, you must first know how much money you are currently spending each month. (Review the Periodic Checkup you completed in Section 5:2.)

Understand that there are monthly expenditures that you may not be able to change immediately, e.g., mortgage/rent and car note, and there are monthly expenditures that you can change relatively easily, e.g., food, clothing and utilities. Focus on the ones you can do something about right now, and implement a budget reduction plan.

With regard to the monthly expenditures you can change immediately, review the amount of money you are currently spending, and try to reduce that amount by 25% the first month. For example, if you are currently spending $300 a month on food, try to spend no more than $225 (or 25% less). Then, after a few months, try to further reduce the amount you are spending to no more than $150 a month (or by another 25%). Keep reducing your budgeted amount until you feel you have decreased this monthly expenditure by as much as you possibly can. Chapter 16 covers ways in which you can decrease the amount of money you spend on food.

The bottom line is that you must establish a budget, stick to it and implement a reduction plan, so that your financial situation won't be left to chance. Having a budget and not sticking to it is just like not having one at all. If you follow your budget and implement a reduction plan by gradually decreasing the amount you are spending in all areas, you can increase the amount you are putting in your savings account.

5:4   Make Budgeting and Saving Rewarding

Every time you save a buck by implementing creative and common-sense ways to save, put it into your savings account. Keep track of the amount of money you are saving. Make sure you use an interest-bearing savings account.

Each month reward yourself by withdrawing only the interest you've earned by saving, and buy yourself something special. Of course, the more you add to your savings account, the more interest you accrue each month.

5:5   Establish at Least One Goal a Month

Since we've established that change isn't easy, a gradual savings approach may be best for you. If so, I've got just the plan: Establish at least one savings goal per month. For example, if one of your goals is to stop eating out so much, then do it.

To keep that monthly goal in practice and fresh on your mind, write it down and stick it on your refrigerator door. Every time you go to the refrigerator, review that goal. Because practice makes perfect, continue to practice your goal of the month until it becomes a habit. Then, establish and begin implementing another goal.

Keep going until you have totally changed your way of thinking financially toward improving your financial condition and becoming totally debt-free. Just think, improving your financial condition can begin by establishing at least one savings goal per month.

5:6   Earmark Your Savings for a Payroll Reduction

Select a certain amount to be deducted from your payroll check and deposited right into your savings account. So, before you ever see it, it's already in there. (If you go and withdraw this money each time you say you need it, then you've defeated the purpose.)

If you can, select a certain percentage of your income, e.g., 20% of your monthly net income or 75% of your monthly disposable income, to deposit. Then, as your monthly debt decreases and your income increases, you should increase the amount going directly into your account. Pretty soon, you will have a nice savings.

5:7　Save! Save! Save!

If you can't start saving 20% of your monthly net income or 75% of your monthly disposable income right now, then start off with less, and gradually increase the amount. By practicing money-saving techniques, you will find extra money during the month that you didn't even know existed.

5:8　Once It's in Savings, Leave It There

A good rule of thumb for us all: Once it goes into your savings account, leave it there. If you make it a habit of withdrawing from your savings for this or that "emergency," then you will have a hard time building up and maintaining an amount in your account to accomplish your long-term financial goals.

When and only when you are ready to complete one of your financial goals, e.g., pay off your car or mortgage loan, should you withdraw the money from your savings. By following this simple rule of thumb, you should expect to accomplish your goals and at a much faster pace.

5:9　Establish a Cash Reserve

A cash reserve is a portion of your income you've saved that you can fall back on if you ever have to. Hopefully, you will never have to, but it is better to have it if you ever need it, than to not have it and really need it.

I recommend that you build up and keep a cash reserve that is equivalent to your living expenses for six months. By doing this, you will have several months to regain financial stability in case of a sudden loss of income.

This money should be liquid, meaning easily converted to cash if you need it. In other words, this money should not be saved in a certificate of deposit. Also, the money should be separate from your other savings account(s) that will be used to accomplish your long-term financial goals. In the event of an emergency, your cash reserve should prevent you from having to withdraw money from your savings account(s) specified to accomplish your financial goals.

In addition to continuing maximum contribution toward your savings account(s) to accomplish your long-term financial goals, you can build up and keep this cash reserve by putting a portion, over and above your regular monthly living expenses and the amount you allocate toward saving, in this cash reserve account. By directing some extra money you would normally spend on clothes or entertainment to your reserve, you will have sufficient money to cover you in the event of an emergency. Although you may not have bought a new outfit for the week or month, by establishing a cash reserve, you have purchased something more important: some peace of mind.

5:10   If You Get a Loan, Repay It Immediately

If you can go through the rest of your life and never have to get another loan, then do it. This is possible once you've become debt-free and have become accustomed to keeping enough money for unexpected expenses.

In the meantime and under limited circumstances, you may have to get a loan. If you must get a loan, make every effort to repay it as soon as possible. By doing so, you will save money because you won't incur any unnecessary interest charges.

5:11   Create Your Own Ways to Save

In this book, I provide you with hundreds of ways to save money. However, as stated in the overview, there are thousands more. It doesn't matter whether you use all of the techniques that worked for me or come up with your own. What does matter is that you develop a plan to save and stick with it until you become 100% debt-free.

5:12   Beware of Financial Planners...

Because they are in the business of making money. Financial advisors may be trying to sell you products and services that make them money at your expense. If you are serious about improving your financial condition, don't get further in debt to receive help. Instead, use free or low-cost information and guidance to assist you.

5:13   Become Organized

In everything you do, become organized. Whether it's implementing some of the ideas mentioned in this book or others, the more methodical you are, the easier you make it on yourself. You will find when you become organized you are bound to save both money and time.

I will be good to myself
by saving money.

CHAPTER 6

Eliminate Credit-Card Debt

6:1   End the Credit-Card Cycle for Good

I know this will be hard for many of us to do, but from this point on, don't use another credit card. Easier said than done, right? Here is the plan:

First, call each credit-card company and ask a representative to lower your interest rate. It costs you nothing to ask.

Second, focus on paying off all of your current credit-card balances by putting all of your money, in excess of your monthly required bills and other necessary expenses (mortgage/rent, utilities, transportation, food) toward your credit-card debts. For the first few months of this process, don't use any excess money for entertainment purposes or to shop. In other words, commit to paying off those credit-card debts you've incurred. Don't stop until you have a zero balance on every credit-card account you have.

Third, cut up your credit cards and throw them away if you think you will become weak and get the urge to charge something you really don't have the money to buy. Don't memorize the numbers either.

Fourth, close those accounts. Be warned that the credit-card companies' representatives will try to convince you to keep the account(s) open. Finally, start living on a cash basis, meaning only buy or charge what you can pay off in full.

6:2   Which Debts Should I Pay Off First?

For motivation, pay off your credit-card debts by starting with the accounts that have the lowest balances. Doing this will give you a sense of accomplishment sooner and encourage you to continue to pay off your other balances.

Another option is to pay off the credit-card debts with higher interest rates or higher account balances. You would pay these off first to lessen the amount of interest charges accrued on debts with higher interest rates or higher account balances.

A third option is to transfer the account balances of credit cards with higher interest rates to those with lower interest. But, make sure the card you are transferring to, especially if it offers a low introductory rate, stays at the lower rate long enough for you to pay off the balance.

One method is motivational, while the others save you money. Whatever method you choose, the most important thing you must do is to keep your focus on paying off all your account balances and don't repeat the vicious credit-card cycle.

6:3   Don't Pay Just the Minimum

If you are serious about paying off your credit-card debts anytime soon, then don't pay the minimum payment. By doing so, depending on the account balance and the interest rate, it could take you forever to pay off that credit-card balance.

According to Stacy C. Notley, president of The Manning Group, Inc., a company of financial planners specializing in credit and debt management in Dallas, if you made a $20 minimum payment on an original credit-card balance of $1,000, having a 19% interest rate, it would take approximately eight years to pay off that balance. By that time, you will have paid almost *double* the original balance. Doesn't that just blow your mind? Unfortunately, by taking this route, it may also blow your chances of achieving financial stability.

Pay as much as you possibly can toward your credit-card account balances so they can be paid off in full at a much faster pace. It will take some sacrificing on your part but, with some effort, you will succeed.

6:4   Charge Card vs. Credit Card

There is a difference between a charge card and a credit card, although the terms are sometimes used interchangeably. A charge card doesn't carry a revolving balance, meaning the entire amount on the account is due upon receipt of the bill. On the other hand, a credit card can carry a balance as long as you have the card, allowing you to pay your balance out over time while incurring interest charges.

With self-discipline, you can use a credit card just like you would a charge card. Just to make it easier on yourself, use a charge card in which you know the entire balance on the account is due at the end of the billing cycle. I recommend this so you won't be tempted to charge more than you can pay at the end of the billing cycle, and thereby incur interest charges and a revolving balance.

6:5   Avoid Credit Cards with Annual Fees

Keep only one credit card, but which one should you keep? There are so many credit-card companies out there, but the answer is simple: Keep the one with no annual fee. For every credit card with an annual fee, there are twenty more without one, so shop around.

6:6   Charge Only Your Necessities

Charge only necessary expenses, e.g., food, gasoline and medical expenses, on your non-revolving credit card, and pay off the balance in full at the end of each billing cycle. By doing so, your money can be earning interest in your bank account until you pay off your monthly credit-card balance and you won't be incurring interest on your debt because you're maintaining a zero balance. In addition, if you receive an itemized list of charges on your monthly credit-card statement, you can keep track of how much you're spending on these bare necessities, and make adjustments to reduce your expenditures, when possible.

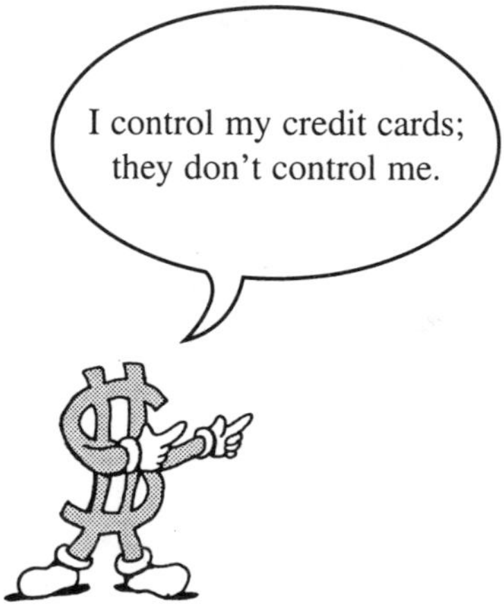
I control my credit cards; they don't control me.

CHAPTER 7

Stop Unnecessary Shopping

7:1   Is Shopping Your Hobby?

If the answer is yes, then let's do some soul-searching. If buying things excites you just as much or more than the items themselves, then re-evaluate your motivation to buy. Shopping, for you, could be an addiction, or something close to an obsession, but you just may not want to call it that. If it is an addiction for you, then seek free counseling or ask a close friend or loved one to assist you in shaking the awful habit.

During the transition of ending your shopping fixation, go to thrift stores or garage sales to satisfy any urge you may have to buy something or just spend money. At least if you do this, you will not be spending as much as you would by shopping at the mall or at retail stores.

You must shake the shopping addiction. If you don't, shopping can be a serious problem that can prevent you from obtaining financial freedom.

7:2   Now that You Know What the Inside of a Mall Looks Like...

You should never have to go again. Trust me, you can go for the rest of your life and not have to make another mall or retail store purchase. I haven't gone to a mall in four years. Now that I know mall shopping isn't a part of life, I keep it that way. You may ask yourself what are you going to do on Saturdays if you don't go to the mall. Be creative, there's more to life than shopping!

7:3   Extreme Moods Could Affect You

Do you go on spending sprees or plan to make a big purchase during times when you are either very depressed or extremely happy? Specifically, when you feel depressed, do you buy something or spend money to make you feel better? Or, when you feel very happy, do you go out and buy something to help you celebrate? If you've answered yes to any of these questions, then the best thing you can do for yourself is to stop and realize that you are hurting your financial condition. Once you are over your emotional low or high, you may find yourself in more debt than before the mood kicked in and that, in and of itself, may make you feel depressed.

Instead of buying something, try doing other things when you get into one of these moods. For example, try exercising when you are depressed, but don't join one of those costly fitness clubs because that entails spending more money. Also, if you are extremely happy about something, expend your "good news" energy by calling your local family members and friends to share your success with them. There are many other ways you can handle mood swings but, by all means, stay away from stores during this time. Once that extreme mood is over, you will be glad you did.

7:4   Don't Be Trendy

Don't purchase clothes, shoes, jewelry, furniture, household furnishings, etc., that you know won't be fashionable within a few months or years. By not being trendy, you decrease the frequency of wanting to make future purchases every time a new trend arises. Remember, trends and fads come and go—the more you try to keep up with the them, the more costly it becomes for you.

7:5 Don't Buy It

Don't purchase something you really don't want or need just because it is on sale or you have a coupon. By doing so, you're wasting your money.

7:6 Beware of Bait-the-Customer Tactics

It is important to mention a growing trend many stores have to bait consumers. This is especially prevalent during holidays. This trend is to offer consumers interest-free/same-as-cash merchandise, which you take home the same day. You can pay out your debt, interest-free, over a specified time and you may not have to make your first payment for months. The retailers offer this easier method of purchase to bait you into buying items you really cannot afford. Think about it. If you have to buy something (other than a house or car) that it takes you approximately a year to pay for, interest free or not, then you cannot afford it. So why buy it?

Here's an alternative: Keep on saving and soon you will be able to instantly purchase whatever you need (or want) and your purchase won't put a dent in your savings account. It may take some time and financial sacrificing to get to this point but, once there, you will enjoy it.

7:7 Limit Network, Catalog and Internet Shopping

Shopping from the television makes it too convenient to spend your money because you never have to leave your house. If you find yourself doing this often, it could become addictive. Also, the products on these networks are usually overpriced and, in addition to the higher costs, you may have to pay shipping-and-handling charges.

Like network shopping, catalogs make it too easy to spend money because all you have to do is pick up the telephone and place your order. Products in catalogs are also overpriced and, in addition to the higher costs, you are often required to pay shipping-and-handling fees.

Thus, eliminate buying unnecessary items using these methods. Also, limit shopping for necessary products, unless you determine that having this convenience isn't costing you more.

For the same reasons I recommend that you limit network and catalog shopping, should you decrease your shopping on the Internet. The bottom line: Stop using any and all methods to shop, especially for unnecessary things. I can't be any more direct than that.

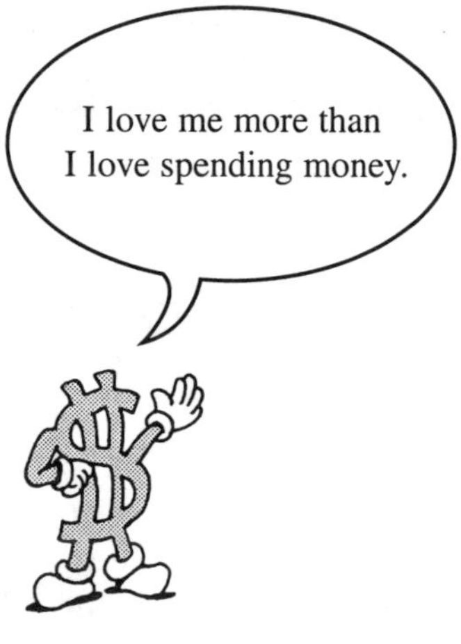
I love me more than
I love spending money.

CHAPTER 8

Effective Ways to Shop

8:1   Don't Buy Some Things Without Coupons

There are just certain things you shouldn't buy without coupons, which are readily available. For instance, you can always find a pizza coupon and you can always find a discount for film developing. These items are priced to offset coupons. Thus, if you don't use one, the company has just doubled its expected profit.

8:2   Don't Do It Just Because You Have a Coupon

Whether you are eating out, buying something at the store or doing something for entertainment purposes, don't do it just because you have a coupon. In other words, don't buy a product you wouldn't normally buy, just because you can get a discount. On the other hand, if you normally eat at certain restaurants or buy certain products, look for coupons.

8:3   Buy What You Need, Not a Label

When you are about to make a purchase, consider whether you are really buying what you need or the designer label. For example, you can buy a regular pair of sunglasses for much cheaper than you can buy a pair of Ray Bans, and they both would serve the same purpose. However, you may want to buy the pair of Ray Bans, just because of the name.

You shouldn't eagerly buy a designer label item and pay two to ten times more than you would pay for it if the name were not on it. Before doing that, compare the quality and determine if paying the extra money is worth it. Don't get caught up in paying for designer labels if there's not a big quality difference and you can buy what you need, with no name, for a whole lot less.

8:4   Stock Up on a Good Deal

When you find a good deal or a sale on non-perishable items you know you are going to need, e.g., toilet tissue, paper towels or soap, be sure to stock up. Designate a closet in your home where you can store these items. Enjoy going to the closet, instead of all the way to the store, as you have a need for these products. If you wait until you need a product to buy it, it may very well not be on sale or you may be tempted to get it at your nearby convenience store, and thus, you may end up paying more for it.

8:5   Buy Generics

Don't buy a product because of its name. Whether you are purchasing over-the-counter medications, shampoos, laundry/dishwashing detergents or any other products in which there are generic counterparts, you may save money if you buy the generic, instead of the brand-name product.

The generic usually costs less. One reason may be due to the companies investing less in the packaging, resulting in a plain or simple look. If you compare the ingredients, however, they are usually the same. Even with the same ingredients, another reason brand names may cost more is because of the costs incurred to advertise these products. These advertising costs are ultimately passed on to the consumer. It makes sense when you think about it. The makers of these products have to compensate for these additional advertising expenses somehow, even though many of the companies who make the brand-name products also make their less costly generic counterparts. Don't be the one to pay for their advertising costs by purchasing the brand name.

Sometimes a brand name for which you have a coupon may cost less than the generic one. Compare costs to determine which purchase saves you money.

8:6   Paying More May Not Mean a Thing

Many people I know truly believe the more the product costs, the better it is. However, some products are more costly based on the popularity of the brand name (usually as a result of advertising), which has nothing to do with quality.

8:7   Compare Cost Per Unit

To ensure you are getting more for your dollar, when purchasing groceries, toiletries or other personal items, compare cost per unit before you buy. Some grocery stores display cost per unit for various products. If the store where you shop doesn't, carry your own calculator so you can figure the cost per unit yourself.

Here's how: Divide the price of the product by the unit, e.g., ounce, gallon or quantity, to determine the price you would be paying per unit. Then compare which price is better per unit. For example, if one brand of ketchup costs $1.29 for twenty-eight ounces and another brand is 99¢ for fourteen ounces, then you would be paying only 4.6¢ an ounce for the first brand and 7¢ an ounce for the second. Although the second brand is cheaper, you are getting more for your dollar if you purchase the first one.

8:8   Watch What You're Charged

While checking out, ensure that you are being charged the correct amount by watching the register. This is not the time to be writing your check, daydreaming, disciplining your children or holding a conversation with the cashier or someone in line. If you are not watching what you are being charged during check-out, then you might be accidentally over-charged.

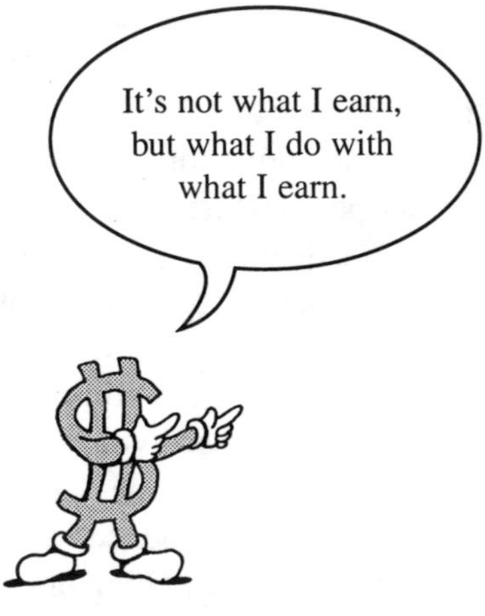
It's not what I earn,
but what I do with
what I earn.

CHAPTER 9

Creative Ways to Buy and Save

9:1   By All Means, Shop at Garage Sales

Shop for anything and everything you need at garage sales. You can find most anything, from clothes and shoes to games, puzzles and electronics, at garage sales. You just have to learn how to find a good bargain. Even if you garage-sale shop, there are limitations. You should budget the amount of money you spend and don't buy anything you really don't need or want just because it's cheap.

Keep these additional pointers in mind: when shopping for clothes, check for visible holes or stains; when shopping for electronics, ask the owner if you can plug in the item to test it before you purchase it; and, when shopping for lawn or exercise equipment, ask the owner to demonstrate the equipment for you.

The best thing about garage-sale shopping is that it doesn't damage your pocketbook as much as shopping at the mall. For the instinctive consumer, you can satisfy any craving you have to spend money by shopping at garage sales, and spend less by doing so.

I usually go garage-sale shopping with my sister or my husband. In addition to clothes, shoes, accessories and other household items we have found for little or nothing, below are some of the best deals we've found at garage:

• ice-cream maker (new)	$2.00
• hard-hat hair dryer (new)	$2.00
• space heater (new)	$5.00
• halogen lamp (slightly used)	$1.00
• digital ear thermometer (slightly used)	$1.50
• bowling ball, shoes and bag (slightly used)	$2.00
• 12-pack, seal-wrapped brand-name deodorant	$2.00
• Christmas decorations (four boxes)	$4.00
• bug zapper (new)	$4.00
• automatic coffeemaker (slightly used)	$3.00
• wood coffee table (good condition)	$5.00
• computer desk with printer stand (good condition)	$25.00
• 29-gallon fish aquarium with wood base/cabinet stand	$18.00
• 19″ color television with remote (good condition)	$30.00
• framed art collection—three 24″ x 34″ (pictures)	$30.00
• 586 computer with CD-ROM (two years old)	$85.00

We still use all of the aforementioned items. I can truly say that garage-sale shopping has been beneficial for us. Give shopping at garage sales a chance, you may like it.

9:2   Don't Believe Garage-Sale Myths

Many people refuse to go to garage sales for a variety of reasons. Common responses I've heard include: garage sales are just for poor folks, items found at garage sales should not be worn by others, and garage sales only have junk even the owner is trying to get rid of.

Well, if you believe any of these myths and won't shop at garage sales, then you are missing out. Lots of people (including myself), who are not poor, find wonderful bargains at garage sales. Clothes can be cleaned and shoes sanitized before wearing them.

Also, garage sales often have items that others need or want and that fit with their style or decor, whereby the previous owner may not have been able to make the same items work for them. We all have different needs, wants and tastes. Just because someone else doesn't like something, doesn't mean you won't, and vice versa. You can go to someone's house today and you will probably find something in their garage that you want and they don't. Before buying into these myths, give garage sales a chance.

9:3   Have Your Own Garage Sale

Gather anything and everything in your home that you don't have a use for, and have your own garage sale. Or, get together with your neighbors and hold a community garage sale to attract more shoppers. Also, check with friends and family members to determine if they have any items they want to donate.

Having a garage sale can be profitable and fun. Just advertise the location, date and time of your sale by printing this information in big, bold print on bright signs and placing the signs out where they are visible, especially on the busier streets around your neighborhood. (Note: Check with the city where you live to determine if there are restrictions on having a garage sale and advertising it.)

Then, the day of your sale, after pricing your items, organize them so they can be easily looked through. Don't price your items too high because in addition to making a profit, you want to get rid of as much as you can during your sale. Start your sale early, say around 7:00 A.M., and have change ready. Once the sale is over, anything you don't sell, donate it to charity and be sure to get a receipt for your donations for tax purposes.

By organizing, advertising and having lots of things to sale, you are sure to make money. Put your earnings in an interest-bearing savings account earmarked to help pay off a debt.

9:4   It Just Doesn't Hurt to Ask

Don't throw away those expired or competitor's coupons just yet. Take them with you and ask the store clerk or manager if you can apply them toward your purchase. The worst they can do is say no. If they do say yes, then you've saved yourself some money. Try it.

9:5   Ask About Referral Benefits

Before you tell someone about a company where you have received good service or a good deal, find out whether the business will compensate you for your referral. You can do so by calling the business. You won't know unless you ask.

Recently, I received good service at a place where I had my car repaired, and when a friend asked where I had the work done, I told her. But before I did, I called the company to ask if they would compensate me for referring a friend. I received a certificate for a free oil and filter change on my next visit, which saved me money. I would have never known had I not asked, but still would have referred had they said no.

9:6   Ask if You Can Buy the Display

If a store will allow you, buy the displayed item for a discounted price. Recently, I was in a store where they had a good sale on a hand-held color television. The store was out of the stocked merchandise and only had the display left. I asked if I could buy the item on display at a discount and return it if it didn't work. Even though the item was on sale, the store allowed me to do so. (Note: Some stores won't sell a displayed item if they are not out of the stocked merchandise, or if merchandise that's not in stock is on sale; they would rather offer you a rain check.)

I negotiated with the store manager to purchase the television for 30% off the sale price. (If you want to purchase a displayed item, some stores will even offer to give you an extended manufacturer's warranty at no charge, instead of giving you a percentage off.) It just so happened that the television I purchased off the display didn't work properly. So, the next week I took the television back to the store and was able to get a brand new one right out of the box, at no additional cost to me.

9:7   Buy Imperfect Appliances and Furniture

Whether you are buying an appliance or furniture, look for ones with small scratches or dents. A store will usually discount these even if the imperfection is minor. Sometimes these items may be the floor models.

I save, not because I love money, but because I love myself.

CHAPTER 10

Things to Know
Before Buying a House

10:1   Buy, Don't Rent

Renting a place to live is like throwing your money down the drain each month. By renting, you can't look forward to one day owning your own property. Also, in many instances, it costs just as much per month to rent a place as it does to buy one; but, by renting, you are not getting the tax benefit you would if you were buying a home. So, why rent? You shouldn't, unless your plans of staying in a particular location or area are short term. Under this limited circumstance, renting a small, inexpensive place, rather than buying a house, makes more sense.

But, if you have long-term plans for staying in a location, then buy a home. You can one day look forward to owning it free and clear, maybe in five years or less, while benefiting from the mortgage interest and property tax deductions.

10:2   Save Three Times Your Down Payment

Before even thinking about buying a house, I suggest that you save at least three times your projected down payment—the estimated total cost due at closing. The reason I suggest saving this amount is so you can equally divide your funds: the down payment; money to purchase appliances, furniture and home furnishings; and enough to maintain a decent savings account.

The last thing you should want to do when buying a house is to go to your mortgage closing with a down payment that depletes your bank account. Also, you should not want to buy a house and either have no money to add the essentials, or feel forced to charge such items just because you did not save to buy them. If you don't have at least three times your projected down payment, you may want to reconsider buying a house right now.

10:3   Financing Your Home

First, look for the lowest possible interest rate you can find and lock it in. Second, determine if there are any mortgage programs for which you may qualify such as bond money for first-time home buyers. Then, finance for as few years as possible, e.g., no more than ten to fifteen years. By doing so, you will save a bundle in interest charges.

10:4   Get Two Liens Instead of One

If you are borrowing more than 80% of the value of your home, then a lender may require you to have private mortgage insurance to protect it in the event you default on the loan. This mortgage insurance premium is added to your monthly mortgage note until the loan is paid down by a certain percentage, usually after one-third of the term of the loan, or the equity has increased by a certain amount either through appreciation or improvement of your property, as determined by your lender. The amount of the premium, also determined by your lender, is based on the amount of your down payment. The smaller your down payment, the greater the premium.

If, for example, the value of the home is $100,000, with a down payment of 5%, a monthly mortgage premium of about $65 would be added to your payments. Using this example, after the first ten years of paying on a thirty-year mortgage, you will have paid almost $8,000 for mortgage insurance.

However, George Fox, president and owner of Certified Mortgage Planners in Dallas explains that if you are unable to put 20% down, you could still get around this cost by getting two liens instead of one, with the same lender. Specifically, he says that you could get a first lien for up to 80% and the second lien for the remainder, minus the down payment. Because the first lien, which is the majority of your borrowed amount, is not more than 80% of the value of your home, then you wouldn't be required to carry private mortgage insurance, and thereby you wouldn't incur this added cost, which is of absolutely no benefit to you.

10:5   'Tis the Season for Home Buying

If you are in the market for purchasing a home, the winter is the best time. Erle Rawlins III, of Real Estate Consumer Consultants in Dallas, who has been practicing real estate since 1968, and representing buyers exclusively since 1990, says that generally home buying increases during the spring and summer. This is probably because most kids are on (or getting ready for) summer break and potential buyers don't have to consider enrolling their kids in a different school or district while school is in session. Also, he suggests that it's easier to look for a home and move in during the summer when the weather is generally better, than it is during the winter. So, if more potential buyers are looking for, and buying homes in the summer, the demand for homes increases, driving up the overall asking prices of homes.

In turn, Rawlins says during the winter, there are less potential buyers because the weather is usually bad and people are shopping for Christmas gifts rather than homes. These factors may lower the demand, and consequently the average selling price of homes. (Note: The increase or decline of interest rates and atypical winter weather conditions may also affect the home-buying market.)

10:6   Keep Emotions Out of Home Buying

If you are in the process of looking for or buying a house, one thing you don't need is for your emotions to get in the way. Erle Rawlins III says that emotional interference can play a negative part for a potential home buyer. If you begin to fall in love with a house (e.g., you begin referring to it as "my house" or you picture where your belongings will go), and the seller knows it, then you've just tossed your bargaining power right out of the window.

Even if you have fallen in love with a house, don't let on. Play it cool. A seller who knows that a buyer has fallen in love with his house may be less likely to negotiate the terms of a contract.

10:7   Don't Buy a House You Will Outgrow

I know many people who buy a house and then a year or two later, they say they have outgrown it. When planning to buy a house, anticipate the current needs and future growth of your family, and whether you have parents or other family members who may come to live with you. You would waste a lot of money if you were to buy a house, only to turn around a year or two later and realize that you need more space.

10:8   Don't Buy More House Than You Can Afford

Lenders use a variety of factors to determine how much you can qualify for to buy a house, including your income, your debt, your credit history and your job stability. The real question is not how much will a lender let you borrow, but how much house can you comfortably afford.

All other factors aside, you should purchase a home for no more than three times your gross annual income. So, for example, if your gross annual income is $40,000, then you should purchase a home for no more than $120,000.

I like this rule, but the cheapskate in me would suggest you buy a house that is no more than *two* times your gross annual income, even if a lender qualifies you for more. So, with a gross annual income of $40,000, you should purchase a home for no more than $80,000.

10:9   If You Want a Pool, Buy a House with One

If you already know you want a swimming pool, then buy a house that already has one. Adding a pool could cost anywhere from $20,000 on up but, once a pool is installed, the value it adds to the house is approximately one-third of its cost of installation. For this reason, let the previous owner pay the rapidly depreciated cost of installing a pool.

I purchased a home that already had an in-ground swimming pool with an attached Jacuzzi, which cost approximately $25,000 to install (and has added only $8,000 to the value of the home). Without the pool, I wouldn't have paid $25,000 less for the house. In other words, my house did not cost $25,000 more than a comparable one without a pool. By purchasing a house that already had a pool, I saved the $25,000 it would have cost to add one.

10:10 Home Buyer Beware

If you are looking to purchase a home and have a real-estate broker working with you to find it, understand that the broker may not be acting in your best interest. Since most brokers represent sellers, that broker is most likely ensuring that the seller of the house will get the most money possible, while no one is ensuring that the potential buyer is paying the least amount.

But, if a broker is driving you around all day and getting to know you better, while looking to sell you a house, you might begin to trust him. If you trust a broker who doesn't represent you, you might release information that may negatively affect your ability to negotiate. Don't be so into buying your home that you overlook this important factor.

Also, be aware that if a broker wants to represent you as a buyer's agent, then make sure he is looking out for your best interests. One of the main roles of a buyer's agent is to make sure you are getting a house for as little money as possible. To do so, the buyer's agent should conduct a thorough market analysis of the house prior to making a recommendation on the amount you should initially offer. The following are some additional strategies a buyer's agent may use to represent your best interest:

- Provide objective opinions about the value, marketability and resale potential of the house

- Determine how long the property has been on the market and how this may affect your bargaining power

- Attempt to find out the seller's motivation to sell the property and any other information that may improve the buyer's bargaining position

- Negotiate a fair price and any other terms of the real-estate contract

- Add clauses to the contract that benefit the buyer

- Get the seller to furnish you with a home warranty

- Negotiate to increase the amount of seller-paid repairs

- Add provisions that benefit the buyer, e.g., making the contract null and void, if it is not expressly accepted prior to a certain date

- Negotiate the closing costs and the date of closing

- Negotiate the amount of earnest money, if any, you put down

- Not reveal anything to the seller or to the seller's agent that could negatively affect your bargaining position

Keep in mind that if you are dealing with a broker, it is important that you, as a buyer, not disclose any information until you know who the broker is representing. If the broker represents the seller as a listing or seller's agent, or if you don't feel that a buyer's agent is truly representing you, then it is important that you, under no circumstances, reveal the maximum amount for which you qualify to purchase a house or any other information that compromises your ability to negotiate the best deal on a house. Also, if the broker is representing the seller (about 90% of them are), then as a buyer, you may want to find a true buyer's agent to represent your best interests.

Nowadays, more brokers than ever, although still less than probably 10%, are in the business of exclusively representing buyers in a real-estate transaction, and even less than that could be characterized as true buyer's agents. A true buyer's agent puts your interests above the agent's own and won't hurry to close a deal just to get paid.

10:11 Assess Your Need for Representation

As a potential home buyer, if you have limited home-buying knowledge, it may be in your best interest to find someone to represent you in the real-estate transaction. You might be able to negotiate with the seller's agent for the seller to pay your buyer-representation fees. In fact, when my aunt and uncle bought a home a couple of years ago, I represented them, and negotiated for the seller to pay my commission. Imagine that: A real estate agent represents you to secure your best interest against the seller, and the seller pays for him to do so. It is not unusual for this to happen.

If you feel you have the knowledge and ability to represent yourself in a real-estate transaction, then do so. By being adequately represented, you are in a better position to make one of the most important purchases that you will ever make.

10:12 Start Negotiations Below Asking Price

If you are in the market for purchasing a home and you are ready to make an initial offer on a home, you may want to consider starting your negotiations below the asking price. However, unless you know there is a compelling motivation to sell, make an offer that you can at least justify value. By doing so, you are in a better position to begin your negotiations. Sellers, when determining an asking price, anticipate that it will be negotiated, which is why sellers usually set asking prices above what they are willing to accept. (Note: This strategy works better when the home-buying market is slow.)

10:13 Make a Strategic Initial Offer

There are several strategies you can use in deciding on an initial offer. Unless the market is extremely hot (meaning houses are selling fast), then you may want your initial offer to be a low one, but not too low that it is not attractive, and thus not taken seriously. One good way to make a lower offer more attractive is to offer to put down a higher amount of earnest money. (Earnest money is a dollar amount a buyer puts down to show his sincere intention to fulfill the terms of a contract, but it is not required to have a valid contract.)

If a higher amount of earnest money is offered, then this may take some of the attention away from the lower offer. For example, if a house is listed at $100,000, offering $90,000 and putting down $10,000 in earnest money, may be just as attractive as making a $98,000 offer and putting down $500 in earnest money. In essence, what you are doing is you are asking for a trade-off—a lower price for your good faith.

The earnest money you put down goes toward the total amount you are paying on a house, so the more you are able to put down, the lower the amount you will owe toward the total purchase price. If, for whatever reason, you default on the real-estate contract, then understand that you would lose your earnest money to the seller, unless a specific term or condition of the contract is not fulfilled, through no fault of the buyer, which nullifies the contract. So don't offer to put down a large amount of earnest money if you feel you may default on the contract.

Another strategy in making an initial offer is to round up. To a seller, a $90,000 offer may sound better than $89,900, although there is only a $100 difference. The opposite applies if you are a potential buyer. For a potential buyer, listing a home for an asking price of $89,900, sounds more attractive to a buyer than listing it for $90,000. Remember, as a potential home buyer, use these strategies and make your initial offer a strategic one.

10:14 It's All About the Equity

The main aspect of home ownership that sellers are trying to get more of, and buyers are trying to pay less of, is the equity—the value of your house, after all liens and other charges against the property have been paid. Simply put, the equity is the home owner's monetary interest in the property.

The amount of equity in a home may be the result of several factors, including making your monthly mortgage payments. As monthly mortgage payments are being made, money is being applied toward the principal of the loan. Hence, the longer you have paid on the loan, the more equity you should have in your home.

Another factor that may influence the amount of equity is the appreciation or depreciation rate of the home. For example, if you bought a home five years ago for $80,000, and more shopping areas and businesses come into your neighborhood causing the area to boom, then the value of your home may appreciate by several thousand dollars. On the other hand, if your neighbors are not keeping up their properties, then this may cause the value of your home to decline, and hence, lower the amount of equity. In addition, the amount of equity may increase because of additions to your house, such as a pool or an extra room, or it may decrease as a result of you not taking care of the home.

Estimating the amount of equity is an important factor for determining the bottom-line dollar amount the owner will accept in selling his home. Thus, it is important for a buyer to try to estimate the amount of a seller's equity, so as to pay as little of the seller's equity as possible. Remember, when buying and selling a house, the equity in a home has a lot to do with the interests of the parties.

10:15 Request a Blind Appraisal

A blind appraisal is one in which there are no external factors to potentially influence the appraised value of a house. During the mortgage lending process, many mortgage companies usually disclose the contract price of the house to an appraiser. As a result, the appraised value is influenced by the amount that's been negotiated for it, and thus, is not based solely on its merits. Therefore, according to Erle Rawlins III, it is important for you to know that, as a consumer, you have a choice to request a blind appraisal.

When I was in the process of buying my home, I didn't know at that time, the potentially negative effects of not having a blind appraisal. Further, I didn't know to request one. It was not until a few weeks prior to closing, when I was chatting with the seller's agent, that he commented, "I'm sure glad the appraiser was able to assess this house for the contract price so this deal would close." I knew then the professional was hired to evaluate the house for the contract price, and not to provide his true opinion, based on his knowledge, research and analysis of the house. (Note: Appraising is not an exact science, so ten different professionals could come up with ten different values for the same house.)

I then realized it was in everyone's best interest but mine, for the house to be valued at the contract price, so the deal would go through. I also realized that an appraiser who is selected by a mortgage company, has a big interest in estimating the value of houses for the contract price, so he can continue to receive business from the mortgage company. This non-blind appraisal of my house facilitated the closing of the real-estate transaction, so that everyone would get paid.

It would have been in my best interest to have had an appraisal conducted by hiring my own independent professional. If I had done so, this person may not have had an interest in whether the real-estate deal would have closed. Hence, the house may have been assessed at a lower value than the contract price. If this would have happened, and with a "subject to the property appraising for not less than the contract price" contingency clause, I could have either voided the contract or renegotiated the deal for the lesser estimated amount.

Or, I could have required, in writing, that the mortgage company not disclose the contract price to the appraiser it appointed. Doing this still may not have guaranteed that the mortgage company would not have disclosed the contract price to the appraiser but, at least, the mortgage company would have been put on notice of my concern.

10:16 Carefully Select an Inspector

It is important to select a good inspector when preparing to purchase a home is what George Fox of Certified Mortgage Planners tells his clients. He explains, a good inspector is one who is thorough and provides the real facts on the condition of the home. A good inspector will be able to identify if there are problems with the foundation, roof, plumbing or electricity, as well as whether there are mechanical deficiencies or termite damage. (Note: A separate inspector may be required for the termite inspection.) Most important, a good inspector will not overlook problems in order for a real-estate deal to close.

It is also important that the potential home buyer and his agent be present during the inspection so you can ask questions, and so the inspector can explain the results to you. By selecting a thorough inspector who has no interest in whether the real-estate deal closes, you are maximizing your potential to know the true condition of a house before you buy it, and minimizing your chances of having unexpected, major problems with the house during the first few years of ownership.

10:17 Ask for Part of the Commission

In most states, there is no law that prohibits a real-estate broker from returning a part of the broker's commission to the principal (buyer or seller) in a real-estate transaction. While there are laws that prohibit a person who is not a real-estate licensee from receiving a commission, paying a rebate to a principal in the real-estate transaction is acceptable as long as all parties to the transaction know and agree to this term.

The reason you would ask for a rebate is because, if it weren't for you, there would be no real-estate commission to be made. This law doesn't require that a broker tell you of your right to receive a rebate, so make sure you ask about it.

Unfortunately for me, I did not know to ask for a rebate when I purchased my home six years ago. As a buyer in Texas, I could have asked the broker for a rebate of the $6,000 commission he made on the deal, and gotten it. Before you buy or sell your property, find out the law in your state regarding receiving a rebate in a real-estate transaction.

10:18 Negotiate Closing Costs

When buying a house, realize that just about *everything* is negotiable.

(Note: There are few exceptions depending on the type of mortgage the buyer obtains.) Although a title company or lender may, in general, suggest who usually pays for certain itemized closing costs, with a few exceptions, it's up to the buyer and seller to make the ultimate determination.

Request a good-faith estimate of your closing costs from your lender or the title company. Then determine which closing costs you want to negotiate for the other party to pay. Or, you can negotiate to pay for no more than a certain amount of the closing costs, and anything over that amount the other party pays. Whether you are a buyer or a seller, negotiate to pay as little as you possibly can.

When I purchased my home, I negotiated for the sellers to pay 2.25 points to lower (buy down) my interest rate by about 2%. (One point equals 1% of the loan amount; usually one to three points may be purchased to lower your interest rate.) They agreed, and this saved me about $2,900 in interest charges. I also negotiated for the lender to waive the 1% loan origination fee, which saved me another $960. If your lender waives some fees, make sure you are not being charged for other things to compensate for the fee waiver.

10:19 Negotiate Miscellaneous Fees

When you are about to close on a mortgage loan, there are several miscellaneous fees, including a loan origination, escrow, courier, documentation preparation, processing, notary, underwriting, wire transfer, etc., for which you may be charged. Your lender or title company should provide you with a good-faith estimate of the closing costs, which may include an itemized list of any of the above-mentioned applicable fees.

Upon receipt of this estimate, review it. Prepare to negotiate for either the seller to pay some of these fees or for the entity—your lender or the title company—to reduce or eliminate some of these fees. Some of these miscellaneous costs are charged to you even though the entity incurred no out-of-pocket expenses.

Also, these fees may be insignificant when compared to the amount of money a lender and a title company will receive just by participating in your mortgage process. Specifically, a lender will benefit by the interest it charges you on the loan and a title company will benefit by charging to prepare and issue you a title insurance policy. Thus, it would be in their best interest to grant your request so they can capitalize in bigger ways.

If a lender or title company won't negotiate to reduce some of these miscellaneous fees, then let them know that you can find others that will—ones that would gladly reduce or eliminate some of these insignificant charges just to have your business. Then, call other companies who will offer you the same or a better deal on an interest rate and the cost to prepare a title insurance policy, respectively, in addition to being willing to negotiate on some or all of the fees. One willing to do so shouldn't be too hard to find. By negotiating with the seller or the entity involved, you'll save yourself some money, and it costs you nothing to ask.

CHAPTER II

Home Ownership

11:1   The American Dream or a Nightmare?

Owning a home was once considered the American dream. But, with so many people foreclosing and falling behind in their mortgage payments, could it now be considered the American nightmare? Well, not exactly.

Home ownership does have some drawbacks: after thirty or so years of paying for a house, you finally own it; if anything breaks down, you are still responsible for fixing it and, after years of paying a mortgage note, you will have paid for the house three times over, once you pay it off. For example, for a $100,000 home, if you use the thirty-year term to pay it off, you will have paid more than $300,000, when all is said and done. That's like going to the store and asking the clerk if you could pay three times the price for an outfit, or asking a waiter if you could pay three times your restaurant bill.

The positive sides to home ownership include: the Internal Revenue Service (IRS) allows you to deduct the mortgage interest and the property taxes you pay on the home, one day you will eventually own the home free and clear and it beats apartment living. So, it could be considered the American dream from this aspect.

Basically, I made it my American dream by implementing the money-saving techniques described here and saved enough to pay off my house. Read Section 11:5, which tells you about my short road to payoff.

You could devise your own quick method of payoff, e.g., doubling or tripling up on the principal. However, if you need further assistance in devising a quick payoff method that will work for you, contact a mortgage planner. Then, just do it. If you make it your goal to pay off your home within five years, as opposed to taking thirty years to pay it off, then you would undoubtedly consider home ownership the American dream.

After paying off your mortgage loan, you won't be able to deduct the interest for tax purposes each year, but owning a home free and clear is a benefit that will save you more money than you will ever be able to recover from the IRS. Look at it this way, on a $100,000 home loan, by paying it off early, you will save yourself nearly $200,000 in interest charges. I guarantee you the IRS won't give you this amount over the next thirty years just by deducting the mortgage interest you've paid. Take it from me, home ownership is the American dream, but paying off your home early makes the American dream worthwhile.

11:2   Determine Source of House-Note Increase

There are several elements that make up a monthly mortgage note: the principal, the interest, the property taxes, the home owner's insurance premium, the mortgage insurance (if you put down less than 20%), and the amount to cover any escrow shortages. If your monthly mortgage note increases, then it is probably due to a rise in your interest rate, property taxes or home owner's insurance.

If you have an adjustable rate mortgage, as opposed to a fixed interest rate, then you should expect your interest rate to increase (or decrease), according to the current interest rates. This type of increase shouldn't surprise you since you should already know what type of mortgage you have. To prevent this type of increase, check into refinancing, and trade in your adjustable rate mortgage for one with a fixed interest rate.

If your house note increases because of the amount of property taxes you owe, or because of your home owner's insurance premium, then you may be able to do something about it. Read Section 11:8 to find out what you can do if your house note has increased because of property taxes. Read Section 27:5 to determine what you can do if your house note has increased as a result of your home owner's insurance premium. Once you determine the source of the increase, it is possible that you can do something about it, and save yourself some money.

11:3   Refinancing May Be an Option

If the interest rate on your mortgage loan is higher (2% or more) than the current rate, you may want to consider refinancing. There may be some closing costs, but try to get them waived, or you may have the option of rolling your closing costs into your loan amount. If this option is available to you, refinancing your home loan, even if you plan on paying it off early, can save you thousands of dollars over the next few years.

11:4   Refinance as a Mental Motivator

After three years of paying on a thirty-year mortgage loan at a 7% interest rate, I reviewed my principal balance and to my surprise, I determined I had only paid $3,000 toward my $96,000 loan. At this rate, it was understandable why I would have twenty-seven more years before my house would be paid off. For an $850 monthly payment, only an average of $80 per month had gone toward my principal loan balance. The bulk of this monthly payment was going toward the accruing interest and the remainder to property taxes, home owner's insurance, mortgage insurance and escrow shortages. So, I decided to do something that mentally motivated me. I refinanced my mortgage loan with a ten-year simple-interest loan.

The refinanced simple-interest loan rate was about the same as the original mortgage loan interest rate. But by refinancing, I was paying only about $100 more a month on a ten-year loan. In addition, the new monthly note, included only the principal and the interest. I was responsible for paying the taxes and insurance myself, when they became due.

When I refinanced, the mortgage company returned the amount that had been escrowed to pay my property taxes and home owner's insurance, which I used to pay the taxes and insurance. In addition, when I refinanced, I asked to waive the loan origination fee, which was 1% of the loan amount. The financial institution agreed to do so if I opened up a checking account with it, which I did. So the only extra cost I paid at closing was for an updated appraisal of my property. I gladly paid for that since I needed a more recent estimate of value for my own records. (To my delight, the appraisal revealed that the value of my home was $15,000 more than the amount I paid for it.)

Actually, it worked out that I was paying about the same after refinancing, as if I had maintained the original mortgage loan and paid an extra $400 a month toward my principal balance. So why did I decide to refinance? For me, to make a payment of only $100 more a month and to know $500, instead of only $80, was going toward my principal balance after each monthly payment, motivated me even more to believe I could pay off my house faster than I ever imagined.

11:5   The Short Road to the Payoff

Here's how I paid off my mortgage loan so quickly:

- During the first three years of owning my home, I deposited the money I was saving by using these techniques directly into my interest-bearing savings account. Once I paid off my car (two years early) and my credit-card debt, I continued saving the extra money toward the payoff of my house.

- After I refinanced for the ten-year term, as I made house note payments, more money was being applied toward the principal amount of the loan, rapidly reducing the loan amount.

- When I received lump sums of money, e.g., IRS refunds, I earmarked these big amounts and paid them directly toward the principal balance of my simple-interest loan. I put any small amounts in my savings.

- During the last year of paying off my house, I continued to deposit the money I was saving from rental income and a variety of other methods directly into my interest-bearing savings account. (Note: The rental income I earned during the last year really helped me pay off my house.)

- While my loan amount was decreasing by a greater amount each month, the amount in my savings was rapidly increasing. When I saved enough money to pay off my house, I withdrew this money and did it! Although I had no money left in my savings once I paid off my house, being totally debt-free enabled me to replenish it quickly.

11:6   Rent It Out

If you don't have children or a lot of uprooting to do, consider moving in with family or friends and renting out your house for a year. Sure, it wouldn't be the most convenient living arrangement, but it's only for a year. Anyone can withstand some inconvenience for such a short, defined period, especially when you use the rental income toward expeditiously paying off your home loan.

Of course, this idea is not for everyone. But if you think it's for you, carefully review the downfalls: you could get bad tenants, you could move in with people you can't live with peacefully, you'd have to find somewhere to store your personal property, you could damage your property while moving and so on. In an effort to avoid some of these downfalls, carefully screen potential tenants, discuss and dissect all aspects of the living arrangement with those whom you are planning to live and iron out any obvious or potential conflicts. It may not be the perfect situation, but it should prove to be economically feasible.

With no children to uproot and after carefully planning the details of this idea for more than a year, I found wonderful tenants and my husband and I moved in with family members. Even with children, we still could have done this. It just would have taken more planning.

After only one year of renting out my house (in addition to implementing other money-saving techniques), I was able to pay off my home loan. In essence, I only sacrificed one year, to own a home free and clear. The situation and rental income worked out so well, my husband and I decided to do it for another year. With all of the extra money being earned and no debts to pay, we plan to build our dream home over the next two years. (See Section 12:1 for details.) Thus, what we had originally thought might be a situation defined by inconvenience, has worked out very well.

Most importantly, this arrangement has netted an income of almost $20,000 a year and has allowed me to pay off my house one year sooner than anticipated. (Note some of the tax implications: During this period, the rental income put me in a higher tax bracket and my home no longer qualified for the homestead exemption, which increased the amount I paid in taxes.) This idea can prove to be very lucrative if you have the flexibility and circumstances to facilitate such a move.

11:7   Get a Roommate or Become One

You can cut your living expenses in half by getting a roommate or becoming one. You don't have to maintain this living arrangement forever, just until you have saved enough money to substantially improve your financial condition.

If you have a house, but you decide to get a roommate to live with you, you can save all the money you are being paid in rent toward paying off your house. Or, if you have not yet bought a house, consider this the most flexible time to cut your expenses by either moving out of your apartment and in with a roommate or staying in your apartment and getting a roommate.

Any way you do it, you can cash in big time by getting a roommate or becoming one. All of the extra money saved could go toward minimizing the time you would have to pay a mortgage, whether you are already buying a house or you are planning to buy one.

11:8   Review Your Property Taxes

As discussed in Section 11:2, the several elements that may make up a monthly mortgage note are the principal, the interest, the property taxes, the home owner's insurance premium, the mortgage insurance and the amount to cover escrow shortages. So, if your property taxes increase, this will cause your house note to increase, unless you pay your taxes separately. Even if your taxes are paid separately, you still don't want to pay more than you have to. Here's what you should do:

The tax-appraisal office in your area periodically conducts appraisals of properties and sometimes values increase. If the tax-assessed value of your home has risen, then your property taxes will increase. If you believe that the increased tax-assessed value of your home is unwarranted, then appeal to your tax-appraisal office.

In preparation for an appeal, be prepared to present any evidence such as structural damage or foundation, plumbing, electrical or roof problems, to justify your belief that the tax-assessed value of your house should be lowered. If it is determined that there are major problems with your house, then the tax-appraisal office may lower its value, and in turn, your property taxes will be lower.

Also, you may appeal the tax-assessed value of your home by comparing it with the value of other homes in your neighborhood. To do a comparison, contact a local real-estate broker and ask him to run a query of the sale prices and square footage of homes that have sold in your area during the last six months. Then calculate the prices per square footage of these homes by dividing their respective prices by their square footage. Next, calculate the tax-assessed value of your home per square footage by dividing its assessed value by its square footage.

If your calculations reveal that the sale prices of homes per square footage are averaging less than the recent tax-assessed value of your home per square footage, then you have a good chance of getting your appraised value lowered, thereby lowering the amount you are paying in property taxes. Review this information to present during your appeal.

If, however, you find that the sale prices of homes per square footage are more than the assessed value of your home per square footage, then you may be out of luck in appealing the increased tax-assessed value of your home. This may be the case unless, of course, you can establish major problems with your home.

Even if you are not appealing an increase, you may protest the value of your home if you believe it has declined over the years, but has remained overvalued according to the tax-appraisal office. If you think the value of your property has declined, protest it presenting the same data as you would for an appeal.

It is important to note that the appraised value of property for tax purposes won't affect the marketability and sales value of your home if you decide to sell it. In fact, one mortgage lender estimated that a current property appraisal for tax purposes may run much less (15% or more) than its appraised value for sales purposes. So, don't be hesitant to ensure that the tax-assessed value of your home is as low as possible, and pay less in property taxes.

11:9   Don't Overlook the Homestead Exemption

If you are a home owner as of January 1 of any given year, then you may qualify for a homestead exemption. This exemption allows home owners to pay a reduced taxable amount on a home that is their *primary* residence.

In addition to the standard homestead exemption, some property tax assessors allow property owners to claim additional homestead exemptions for their primary residence. For example, home owners who turn sixty-five years old during the year, or as of January 1 of any given year are disabled, or are over age fifty-five and a surviving spouse of a person who received the over-sixty-five exemption, may qualify for additional property tax reductions.

Don't expect to receive any of these homestead exemptions automatically. When you first buy a home that will become your primary residence as of January 1, or you turn sixty-five, or you become qualified as of January 1 for the other aforementioned exemptions, you must apply for a homestead exemption. If you don't, you may not receive the exemption for your home, which results in you paying more in property taxes.

11:10 Selling Your Home?

You already know that most brokers have the seller's best interest at heart. Buyers are often on their own. This is why I have dedicated a whole chapter to buying a home, and only a section to selling a home. Here are a few pointers for the seller:

- If you want to sell your home, sell it for the maximum amount you can possibly gain, while minimizing your expenses.

- Assess whether you can effectively sell your home yourself, without the use of a real-estate broker. The library and bookstores have a number of books about selling a home to assist you. If you can sell your home yourself, this will save you thousands of dollars in commissions.

- Before determining an asking price, research the market by finding out the amount for which comparable homes in your area have recently sold. A real-estate broker may assist you in doing this, possibly for free. You do not want to set an asking price that is too low because, by doing so, you have just reduced the amount of your return on the sale; on the other hand, if you set a price that is too high, then you may have a hard time selling your property.

- Set an asking price that is above the bottom-line offer you will accept, so there is room for negotiation.

- Place a "for sale" sign in your yard. This is not only the cheapest way to advertise, but it attracts the attention of those who weren't (or didn't know they were) in the market to buy.

- Advertise your home in the newspaper. It is a cheap way to draw those who are in the home-buying market.

- Schedule and advertise (in the newspaper) an open house. Sunday afternoons draw the most potential buyers.

- When showing your home, make sure your house is neat, clean and looking its best, inside and out. Nothing prevents the sale of a house more than a tacky or nasty appearance.

- Offer the buyer a home warranty. A home warranty is a policy that assures the buyer of mechanical, plumbing and electrical repairs in the home for a specified period. It usually costs about $300 to $500, and is a cheap way to make the sale of a home more attractive.

- Negotiate to pay as little as you possibly can for closing costs and repairs.

- Put your home up for sale beginning in March or April. More buyers are beginning to look for homes as summer approaches.

- If you use a real-estate broker to sell your house, make sure the agent doesn't reveal any information that may lead a buyer to conclude that you are desperate to sell. Some real-estate agents run off at the mouth and unintentionally disclose information about the seller's position that the seller may not have authorized him to disclose. This could negatively affect the seller's bargaining position.

- Review Chapter 10.

By selling your home yourself, you will save a bundle of money. But, don't hesitate to hire a real-estate broker if you don't feel comfortable with your knowledge about selling a home.

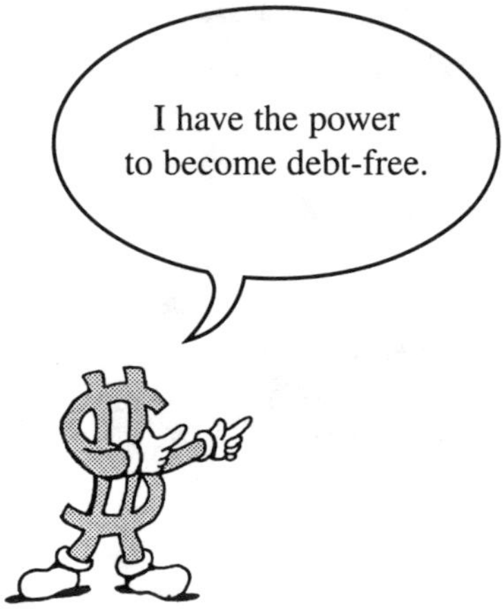
I have the power
to become debt-free.

CHAPTER 12

Home Building,
Repairs and Maintenance

12:1   Be Your Own General Contractor

If you don't own a home, or you already have a house, but want to have another one built, consider serving as your own general contractor. By doing so, you will find and buy a piece of property, secure the building permit, pay for the costs of materials and labor to build your house and coordinate the whole building process yourself. This way, you'll know almost to the penny, the actual costs of building your own house. You may discover that you could build a house for about one-third less than you'd pay for a comparable house.

There is a lot more involved in serving as your own general contractor than can be touched on in this section. Make sure you review all of the available resources you can find on how to serve as your own general contractor, in addition to these money-saving suggestions:

- Realize that preparation is the key. Visit a library or bookstore to find books regarding how to be your own general contractor. Watch television programs about home building/improvements. Talk to others you know who are not general contractors who have successfully built their own homes. While talking to them, take extensive notes. They may not only provide you their personal home-building experience, but they may also be able to recommend subcontractors who did good jobs for them at the most reasonable costs.

- Find a piece of property you can readily build on, so you won't have to pay just to get a property up to building code standards before you start.

- Negotiate to pay as little as you possibly can for the property you want to buy. Instead of financing the piece of property, pay cash if possible, so you can avoid the interest charges of a loan.

- Try to find an architect who has a set of stock blue prints that you like and buy them because they are cheaper, instead of paying an architect to design a whole new set, which can be expensive. If you can't find a set of prints you like, select a set that is close to a design that you like and have the architect make alterations from that set. Also, make sure you submit all of the requested changes you want made to the blue prints at the same time because you may be charged for subsequent changes.

- Make sure the blue prints meet building and city code requirements and that they don't violate any subdivision restrictions for the city in which you plan to build. Also, make sure the blue prints meet all of the minimum side and frontage lot requirements for the specific piece of property.

- Find a building supply store employee that will do a take-off for you for free. A take-off is when an experienced building supply store employee creates a comprehensive materials list based on the study of your blue prints. This service could cost you anywhere from $300 to $400 on up, but some stores will provide you this service at no charge, in hopes that you will buy all of your building materials from them. Even if you find a store that will do a free take-off, if it doesn't provide you the best estimates, don't be compelled to buy your materials from it.

- Once you have a comprehensive materials list, give copies of it to different lumber yards so they can give you estimates for your materials. (Note: From the take-off, type your materials list so one lumber yard won't know the other's estimates.) Compare your overall estimates to determine the best one. Then, compare your materials list, line by line, for each store where you have obtained an estimate.

- Purchase all of your building materials from the store that gives you the best overall estimate. For certain items that are listed at a higher price at the store in which you will purchase your materials, ask if the store will match a competitor's lower price for the same item, plus give you an additional discount. (Note: The building process is complicated enough, so even if a store doesn't match or beat a competitor's price, I would not recommend you get your building materials at several stores because you find that an item is cheaper, unless the difference in price of the item is substantial to you.)

- Negotiate for free and as-needed delivery of your materials. When purchasing such a large order, most stores will deliver your materials at no charge as you need them. Don't forget to ask for this service.

- Avoid getting a construction loan to pay for the building materials and labor costs, which would be accompanied by a lot of interest charges. Find out from the city in which you plan to build if it has requisite time frames in which you'd have to comply to build your home. If it doesn't, or if its time frames are flexible, build only as much as you can afford to pay for in cash. (Note: Continue to save money until you are financially ready to move to the next phase of the building process.) Or, in a city with more stringent time frames for home builders, don't start the building process until you have saved enough to get as far along in the process as needed to meet the city's requisite time frames.

- Get at least three estimates for lot preparation or tree removal, if you need this type of work. (Most cities will allow you to do all lot preparatory work and tree removal prior to applying for your building permit.) The same person may give you a higher bid for the lot preparation and a lower bid for the tree removal, or vice versa. Depending on the estimates, you may want to use two different subcontractors to complete this dual job. Or, go with a subcontractor who has a lower estimate for one part of the job and request that the subcontractor lower his price of the higher estimate.

• Consider purchasing a builder's risk policy to insure your structure during the building process. Shop around for the best insurance policy rates. Also, understand that there are limitations for these types of policies. Inquire with an insurance agent.

• For the entire building process, prepare to get estimates for the materials only and for the labor only. This way, you'll be able to pinpoint these costs separately. Start getting these estimates early.

• You should also get estimates from electrical, plumbing and mechanical (air conditioning/heating) subcontractors early. Usually, a city requires you to supply the names of the aforementioned subcontractors you are planning to use when you submit your application for a building permit. You may want to check with the city as to whether you can change a listed subcontractor, if necessary, during the building process. However, to lessen the likelihood of changing subcontractors, acquire enough information early on to make a decision regarding the subcontractors you plan to use.

• Get at least three estimates for each type of subcontractor. If your estimates are all based on the same criteria (e.g., cost of labor per square footage), it should be easy to compare estimates and determine which are best. Select the subcontractor with the lowest estimates provided his references check out and you've had a chance to review some of his work.

• Purchase concrete and have your slab poured during the winter. Charles Taylor of Taylor & Associates Concrete Supply in Dallas, Texas, has been in the concrete business for twenty-six years, and says that concrete is usually cheaper in the winter and the demand for concrete workers is also lower then.

• Buy your lumber during the winter. Steve Hibbard, who has been in the business of selling lumber for more than ten years says that lumber is also usually cheaper if purchased in the winter. Since most lumberyards won't allow you to store the wood there, be prepared to start the framing process soon after you make your purchase. Also, framers may offer to do your framing for less during the winter because the demand is usually lower then.

- Make sure every aspect of the building process will meet the city's building code specifications before starting any phase. There is nothing more expensive and more frustrating than completing a phase of the building process only to have to redo it because it didn't pass city and code specifications.

- Prior to beginning any phase of the building process, have each subcontractor itemize what all of their work will entail and cost. If this information is not in writing, then you increase your chances of having misunderstandings regarding what specific work the subcontractor was hired to do and what work was to be included in the cost of the estimate.

- Upon satisfactory completion of each subcontractor's work, and once the final payment is made, require each subcontractor to sign a release of lien—a document signed by both parties that the work the subcontractor was hired to perform has been completed and full payment has been made. A release of lien lessens the likelihood of a subcontractor erroneously placing a lien on your property alleging non-payment for work performed. You can prepare a release of lien yourself just by indicating that all work hired to be performed was completed and the subcontractor was paid in full.

- Don't pay a subcontractor in full for work not yet performed. As we all know, everyone isn't honest. For each subcontractor, negotiate to pay in stages with the final payment due upon completion of work performed, not before.

- Avoid hiring subcontractors from big businesses; they usually charge more than subcontractors from the smaller ones. Instead, look in thrift papers or drive around a neighborhood where new homes are being built to find independent, smaller companies to do the work. Sometimes you can even find someone who works for a big business to do the job on the side at a more reasonable price than what a big business would charge you.

• Realize that a lot of hard work goes into serving as your own general contractor and that it is not going to be easy. Be prepared to put in the time. Also, understand that you will make some mistakes during the process. But, when all is said and done, it will all be worthwhile.

12:2   Do Your Own Handiwork

Whether your house needs painting, wallpaper, light fixtures or ceiling fans, do it yourself or have a family member or friend to do it for you for free. There are just some things you don't need to pay someone else to do. If you don't think you can do it and don't know anyone who can, then visit a home improvement store. Many offer free advice and classes on how to do your own handiwork. Also, watching home improvement shows or borrowing books or videos from the library may be helpful.

12:3   Try Doing Your Own Repairs First

If something breaks down in your home, before calling a repairman, try repairing it yourself. By trying your hand at fixing the problem, you may be able to save some money.

Let me share my experience: A while ago, I was faced with a non-working garbage disposal and two toilets that wouldn't stop running. I called a plumber and he gave me a rough estimate of $300 just to replace the garbage disposal. After hearing that, I decided my husband and I would attempt to conquer the job ourselves. First, we went to a home improvement store and purchased a garbage disposal and the parts to repair the running toilets. The total cost for all of the parts was about $50. While at the store, we talked to some experienced store employees who told us step by step how to replace the garbage disposal and how to fix the running toilets. The store employees were both knowledgeable and helpful and the information and instructions they provided were priceless.

We got home and successfully completed all of the repairs ourselves. We were so excited—I don't know if it was about saving the repair costs or about our amazing ability to do what we at first thought we couldn't do. Nonetheless, doing our own repairs gave us some sense of accomplishment and netted a savings of at least $250 in repair costs as well.

12:4   Before Hiring a Subcontractor...

Solicit bids from no fewer than three. Sometimes vast differences in bids are the results of length of warranty on the work performed, quality of supplies used to do the work, different methods or procedures in doing the work, etc. Ask the bidder to itemize the costs that make up the total amount of the bid. Once you understand the costs, then you are in a better position to determine which subcontractor to hire.

If you find that the main or only difference between bids is that the higher ones are likely due to the company's name, reputation or higher overhead costs, then consider going with a lower-bidding subcontractor. But, if you find that the lower bid is due to aspects such as the use of lesser quality supplies, then determine whether this factor will affect the overall longevity and quality of the work performed. In addition, don't forget to ask each subcontractor for references and call their references. This will also assist you in deciding which subcontractor to hire.

12:5   Clean and Service Your Own Pool

If you have a swimming pool and have ever paid to have it cleaned or serviced, then you know that pool companies charge you an arm and a leg. In an attempt to find ways to cut my monthly expenses after I got married, my husband and I decided to learn to clean the pool ourselves. Here's how we learned:

First, we bought the supplies we needed. In turn, the experienced store employees sat with us for four hours and taught us everything we needed to know about cleaning and servicing a pool. We chose this company because they didn't service pools in our area and had nothing to lose by teaching us how to do it. I took extensive notes during the session and subsequently typed up these notes to put on the refrigerator door as our reference. I also wrote these employees' telephone numbers down so we could call them in the event we had some additional questions.

12:6   Get Pest Control Services as Needed

Many people who need an exterminator, sign a contract. Instead of using a company that requires you to be under a contract, find one that will allow you to use their services on an as-needed basis. Then, you can schedule and pay for pest control services as you need them.

12:7   If You Are Buying It, Take Care of It

Some people put their hard-earned money into buying a home, only to tear it up or allow their children to do so. This may seem like common sense, but I'll offer it anyway: If you are buying your home, it is important that you make a conscious effort to take extra-special care of it. Why? Because it's yours, and it's probably one of the biggest investments you will make over your lifetime.

12:8   If You're Not Buying It, Don't Fix It Up

Unless you are buying your home or you already own it, don't fix it up to suit your specific tastes. For example, if you are renting, don't change the wallpaper or the fixtures in the kitchen and bathroom just because you don't like them. Time after time, I see people making these and other changes or improvements to places they don't even own. Save that money. Then, when you are buying your own home, make any changes or improvements you desire. Of course, do so frugally.

12:9   In a Home Owner's Association?

If you live in a neighborhood that is part of a home owner's association then, chances are, you are paying association dues, which can amount to more than several hundred dollars a year. As an alternative to coming out of your pocket to pay dues, ask the association if you can "work them off." I've known some associations to allow its members to work off their dues by planting flowers, mowing the grass and doing any other tasks to beautify the association's building and its surrounding area. By doing so, you would also be beautifying your own neighborhood. If the association does not already have this type of system in place, maybe you can suggest it.

I can be anything
I want to be,
including debt-free.

CHAPTER 13

Household

13:1   Do Your Own Dirty Work

Wash your own car, clean your own house and mow your own lawn. Before it became common to pay someone to do these things for us, we did them ourselves. Now we have gotten spoiled, not to mention sedentary. But realize that by doing your own dirty work, you can kill two birds with one stone. According to one report, cleaning a house burns more than 300 calories per hour, washing a car burns more than 350 calories per hour and mowing a lawn burns more than 400 calories per hour. You can get a good workout and save money.

13:2   Warranties: Could They Spell Rip-off?

Whether you are purchasing a television, VCR, video camera, telephone, washer, dryer, refrigerator or dishwasher, you may find that the additional cost for the manufacturer's extended warranty is not cheap. An appliance or electronic equipment sometimes comes with a one-year manufacturer's warranty, usually at no extra cost. A salesperson may offer to sell you an extended warranty, but don't be so ready to give up the extra money just yet.

Before purchasing an extended warranty, consider several factors. First, the chances of a brand-new appliance/electronic equipment breaking down within two or three years of purchase are slim. Although there is no guarantee you have purchased a product that is flawless, if you have taken good care of it, the odds of a new product breaking down are still in your favor.

Second, understand there are limitations to warranties. For example, if a company determines that you are responsible for an equipment breakdown, you may not be able to have the item repaired or replaced by it at no charge.

Third, you should determine whether the cost of the warranty is unreasonably priced. For some of the low-cost items such as coffeemakers, cordless telephones and other smaller household appliances, determine whether the price of the extended warranty is more than you would pay to replace the item after the warranty is up. For big-ticket items such as refrigerators, washers and dryers, determine whether the warranty is more than it would cost you to find a repairman to fix the item, should it break down during the time of the warranty. If so, it may not be beneficial for you to purchase the extended warranty.

13:3   My Favorite Kitchen Savers

There are many ways you can save in the kitchen, but here are a few of my favorites:

• Cook enough for leftovers. If you are preparing a meal, it may only cost a few cents more to cook enough for seconds—or thirds.

• Dilute carbonated drinks with water. Younger kids don't have to know it and, by doing this, you are not only stretching the amount you have, but you are also being considerate to your kids' kidneys.

• Cut or tear your paper towels in half, especially for your kids' use, so that your roll of paper towels will last twice as long. Manufacturers also make some paper towels now with smaller, perforated sections.

• Reuse sandwich bags, foil, wax paper, paper plates and cups when possible.

Whether you use all or only one of my favorite kitchen savers or you have some of your own, you are bound to save money each time you do. Now that makes a lot of "cents."

13:4 Throw Away that Junk Mail

Make it a habit of discarding all junk mail. Start by immediately getting rid of all credit-card offers you receive by mail. Then, toss any junk mail sent to entice you to purchase things you really don't need. (Buy one of those inexpensive paper shredders to avoid a bigger problem of fraud.) The bottom line: Stop accepting offers just because you receive them in your mailbox.

13:5 Use Grocery Sacks as Trash Can Liners

Instead of buying garbage bags, use grocery bags or sacks to line your trash cans. The plastic bags can be used for small trash cans and the paper sacks are good for the bigger receptacles.

13:6 Use Paper Towels Less and Cloth More

Whether for your bathroom or kitchen, make an effort to use paper towels less and cloth towels or sponges more. The more paper towels you use, the more you have to buy. Although cloth and sponges may be less sanitary because they are reusable and tend to hold germs, use them, when possible, so you can buy less paper towels.

13:7 Frame It Yourself

Professional framing can sometimes cost more than the actual work you are having framed because there is an "art" to framing. You can learn this art by visiting a gallery that does framing and picking up pointers from professionals. The professional framers may offer you suggestions on the colors and types of frames and mats to use.

Once you've gotten ideas from the framing professionals, go to an arts and craft store and purchase your own supplies. Then, frame your own artwork, pictures or paintings yourself, and no one will ever know it wasn't done by a professional, or that you didn't pay to have it done unless, of course, you choose to tell them.

13:8   Make Your Own Floral Arrangements

You can save a bundle while expressing your creativity by making your own artificial floral arrangements. Visit a store that sells them to get an idea of what you like. Then, you can decorate your entire home with beautiful ones you create. Here's how:

Buy a vase. Then find some flowers that match the decor of the room where you want your arrangement. You can use Styrofoam to hold flowers steady in a vase that you cannot see through; you can use marbles, which add to the décor, to hold flowers in a transparent vase.

Buying prearranged flowers can cost anywhere from $35 on up. So, have fun and save by creating your own floral arrangements.

13:9   Paying for Storage: Keep It Temporary

Many of us need to store things, and we often have to pay for storage. However, some of us use storage as a permanent residence for our stuff. Paying storage fees, if you must, should only be temporary (no more than six months).

If you are moving in with someone for a year or more, determine whether the value of the items you are storing is worth more than your storage fees. Your fees shouldn't amount to more than the items are worth. As an alternative to paying these fees, determine if you have a friend or family member who has room for you to temporarily store your belongings.

CHAPTER 14

Utility Bills

14:1   Utility Bills Don't Have to Be Expensive

Heating and cooling costs could account for nearly half of your utility bills. Thus, constantly running your central air or window unit is like throwing money down the drain. To cut your utility bills, give your unit a rest, when possible. If you have children, family members with health problems or indoor pets (or if there is a heat wave or freezing spell), then you may exercise this money-saving idea, but with extreme caution and consideration of the needs of others.

To decrease your utility bills during the cooler summer days, use ceiling and portable fans or open your windows and screened doors. At night, turn off the unit and use light bedding.

To decrease your utility bills during warmer winter days, turn on portable electric heaters for only the rooms of the home that are in use and sleep under an electric blanket. Never leave electric heaters on unattended and never place them near drapes or any other flammable material.

By using these techniques, my utility bill averages around $60 a month for my 2,200-square-foot home. Some of my neighbors, with comparable houses, admitted that their utility bill ranges from $175 to $300 a month. By having lower bills, I deposited the extra money saved in my account earmarked to pay off my mortgage loan. The savings here was more beneficial to me than having a perfectly cooled/heated home year-round.

14:2   Sometimes Change Is Good

Changing the filter in your central air unit either once a month or as often as necessary can lower your utility bill by 10% to 20% per month. By not changing the filter, your unit has to run extra hard because the filter is dirty.

14:3   Be Timely, Decrease Your Utility Bills

You don't have to take thirty-minute showers or have a "mini pool" bath to get clean. You can take a good shower and wash your hair at the same time in less than ten minutes. In addition, you can also take a good bath without full submersion in the water.

If you or someone in your household enjoys long showers or mini-pool baths, encourage them to conserve water and energy. By using less water, you may lower your water bill. You may also lower your utility bill a few dollars each month by using less of the energy (gas or electric) it takes to heat your water.

14:4   Other Ways to Be Energy Efficient

There are several ways you can be energy efficient:

• If you have rooms that are not being used, close the vents. This way, air conditioning or heat is not being wasted to control the temperature in these rooms.

• Once you exit a room, turn off the lights, the television and anything else that uses electricity. Teach your children and others in your household to do the same.

• Replace a regular showerhead with a water-saving showerhead. This saves you thousands of gallons of water each year. This also means a reduction in your water bill.

• Wait until the dishwasher is full before running it. If you don't, then you are wasting both water and electricity. Also, once the dishwasher is full, run it on the lowest or most energy-efficient cycle.

• Prior to washing a load of clothes, make sure you have a full load. If you have several small loads, try to group some of them together so you will have fewer and larger loads to wash.

I don't deserve to be confined by money.

CHAPTER 15

Telephone Bills

15:1   Write, Write, Write

Take time to write your long-distance friends and family members to catch up on what's been going on. I know it's hard to write when it's easier and takes less energy to pick up the telephone and call, but if you catch up on the telephone, you may find yourself with a sky-high bill.

If you must call long distance, here are some tips to follow: shop around for the long-distance plan that suits your calling pattern, only call those long-distance pals when discounts are being offered or, if you already have a cellular telephone, check into a plan that offers free long distance.

15:2   Say Good-bye to Telephone Options

Have you ever seriously taken a look at all of the options you've added to your basic monthly telephone service? Well, if not, do so as soon as you get your next telephone bill. Determine whether you really need those costly options: anonymous call rejection, auto redial, call block, call forwarding, selective call forwarding, call return, call trace, call waiting, priority call, three-way calling and caller ID. More than likely, you don't really need all of these options, which can increase your monthly telephone bill by up to 60%.

15:3   Get an Answering Machine

Get rid of telephone company voice mail, which may cost you about $8 a month, indefinitely. Instead, buy an answering machine, which you may only have to purchase once every few years. If you continue to maintain voice mail, over the next twenty years, you will have paid about $2,000, provided the rates never increase, which is highly unlikely. For that amount, you could buy about fifty answering machines.

15:4   Make the Call on Them

Many companies that are not in your area usually have toll-free telephone numbers. Before calling any out-of-town or out-of-state companies directly, find out if they have a toll-free number. The directory assistance number for toll-free listings is 800-555-1212. The service is free and you can use it as often as you like.

However, if after calling directory assistance, you find that a particular company does not have a toll-free number, call the company directly and ask a representative to call you back. Companies with good customer service are usually willing to pay for the call since they want your business. Besides, why should you foot the bill when those companies can afford to pay for those long-distance calls more so than you?

15:5   Limit Your Use of Directory Assistance

If you are able to get to your telephone directory and look for a telephone number, then don't use directory assistance because it is not cost effective. Instead, keep a personal telephone book of the telephone numbers of people and businesses you call regularly whose numbers you can't remember. This should assist you in minimizing your use of directory assistance.

Also, some local telephone companies offer directory assistance at no charge for individuals who have disabilities that prevent them from manually looking up telephone numbers. If you feel you may qualify for free directory assistance, call your local telephone company to inquire whether it offers this service.

15:6   Cut Cellular Telephone Costs

Nowadays most people have a cellular telephone. But, do you really need one or do you just want one? Only you can answer this question. I will suggest that if you don't already have a cellular telephone, then you probably don't need one, so don't get one.

But, if you have a cellular telephone and don't want to get rid of it, or if you're thinking about getting one because you feel you need it for emergencies, then determine how you can have your phone and save money. Ron Gautreaux, owner of Vital Communications, has been selling cellular phones for fourteen years. He offers these ways to make your cellular telephone use more cost effective:

• Realize that not all plans are alike. There are plans for the low-user and the high-user. Assess which type you are.

• Inquire with your carrier at least quarterly, to keep abreast of the newest and latest changes on rates (and equipment), and how these rates may save you money.

• Learn how to read your bill. Most bills come with itemized charges; you can determine which features you can do without and which ones save you money.

• Be aware of your rate plan so you can use your phone only during non-peak hours (when the rate per minute is either free or less costly), with the exception of making emergency calls. If you find that you are using your phone more during certain times of the day, determine if there is a rate plan for your use pattern.

• Inquire about services such as long distance, caller ID, voice mail and call waiting. Some companies offer them for free. A cellular long-distance service may eliminate your need to make long-distance calls from your home phone, and caller ID and voice mail may eliminate your need for a pager.

- If you don't wish to limit the number of cellular phones to one per household and don't want to share its use, some companies have plans that allow you to add a second phone (and line) to the same account for less than it would cost you to get a phone in a new account.

- Some companies offer phone-to-phone plans, which allow you to talk to other cellular phone users and not incur airtime. Assess whether you need this service.

15:7   Don't Call Psychic Hot Lines

Ever thought about calling one of those psychic hot lines to receive a reading? Well, stop thinking about it. Psychic hot lines may try to bait you in as a frequent customer by giving you a few minutes free. But, one news report I saw indicated that even with those free minutes, the average cost of one of these calls is $49.

In addition, those psychic hot-line advertisements indicate that the calls are "for entertainment purposes only." Since this is the case, I'm sure you can find less expensive ways to entertain yourself. Also, these hot lines tend to play upon the emotions of depressed or distraught people by giving them good readings. The more good you hear, the more you are likely to call back. And, of course, the more you call back, the more these psychic hot lines profit.

One positive thing is that most ensure confidentiality because you don't know the person on the other end of the phone and they don't know you. But, confidentiality doesn't have to be this costly. Instead of paying for confidentiality, go to a trustworthy friend, your pastor or anyone you trust who has the time to listen and talk to you. Or, if you feel the need to talk with a psychic, to avoid those expensive hot-line costs, find a place where you can get your palm read for $5.

15:8   Say No to Telemarketers

It seems as if telemarketers know when you get home, get comfortable and are about ready for dinner because that's when they start calling. Whether it's a credit-card offer or any other kind of promotion, their goal is to get you to spend money. Say no to their offers—not just because they have interrupted your day, but because, even though the offer may sound great, it will cost you if you accept it.

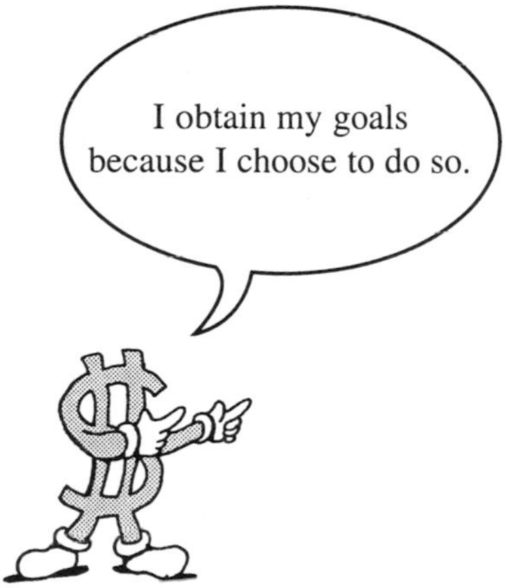
I obtain my goals
because I choose to do so.

CHAPTER 16

Food and Beverages

16:1   Eat Breakfast at Home

It is less expensive to have your coffee, orange juice, bagel or cereal at home than to buy breakfast out. You can buy a package of bagels or muffins and an eight-ounce container of cream cheese for almost as much as you'd pay for one bagel and a single-size serving of cream cheese, eating out. Also, you can drink several servings of juice for less than you'd pay for one glass while eating out.

So, the next time you are making out a grocery list, add some breakfast foods to it. You may have to wake up a little earlier to prepare your meal but, think of it this way, by doing this rather than eating breakfast out, you'd probably save hundreds of dollars a year.

16:2   Take Your Lunch

Make it a practice to take your lunch to work and have your children take their lunches to school. Stock a variety of foods so you and your family won't get burned out on that same old sandwich. Also, instead of buying a variety pack of chips, which costs more, buy one big bag and separate the chips yourself into individual-size portions. Do the same for cookies and other snacks.

16:3   Keep a Stash

When it's not too hot and chances are low that soft drinks may explode, keep a stash of soft drinks in your car for when you stop at fast-food restaurants. You can often purchase a six-pack of soft drinks on sale for less than the amount of money you would spend if you bought a large soft drink at a fast-food restaurant. Some places will even give you a cup of ice and a straw if you ask for them when ordering your food.

Also, many restaurants offer value meals, which come with sodas. Determine whether it's cheaper to get the value meal. Another way to save is to drink water, which is free at a lot of places.

16:4   Stick to It

Once you've made your grocery list, go shopping and stick to the list. Also, make less frequent, scheduled trips to the store because the more often you go, the more you tend to buy. In addition, never go to the store when you are hungry because studies have shown that grocery shoppers tend to buy more and buy on impulse when hungry, which makes it even harder to stick to your list.

16:5   Discount Grocery Stores

Discount grocery stores do exist, you just have to find one in your area. These are stores that offer slightly dented canned goods and food and other products with fast-approaching expiration dates, at discounted prices. These types of stores could provide an alternative and very economical source to shopping at a regular grocery store.

16:6   The Bigger, the Better?

There are instances in which I know bigger is better—a better value, that is. Buying condiments and paper goods, for example, are often a better value if bought in larger portions or quantities.

16:7   Buy Meat in Bulk

Buy the larger-quantity packages of meat. Then, soon after getting home from the store, tightly repackage the meats in freezer bags or freezer paper into portions that fit the size of your family or appetite.

16:8   Ever Have Leftover Meat or Poultry?

Well if you do, I have a great idea. Instead of throwing it out, reinvent. Turkey and chicken are great for turkey or chicken salad sandwiches or even homemade pot pies. (You may find a great pot pie recipe on the back of soup cans.) Roast tastes terrific in stew, and brisket can reappear as beef on a bun. By finding creative ways to use leftover meat and poultry, you are less likely to be tempted to go out for lunch or dinner, which can be expensive.

16:9   Bottled Water Shouldn't Be Costly

These days, more and more people prefer drinking bottled water, which can be a costly drink if considerations are not given when determining how you will purchase it. Instead of buying or renting a water cooler and having your bottled water delivered to you or buying small bottles, buy a refillable one- to three-gallon container of water, and for approximately 35¢ a gallon, take it to the store where you can get refills as often as necessary, then refrigerate it at home. Refill the smaller bottles when needed. Of course, this is not as convenient as having the water delivered to your home or buying individual bottles of water, but it's worth a little inconvenience for the money you'll save.

16:10 Roll in the "Dough"

A loaf of bread has gotten pretty expensive. I remember when bread was about 59¢ a loaf. Depending on your age, I'm sure some of you can remember when it was a nickel a loaf. Bread makers have discovered that we need them, so their prices have increased faster than inflation.

Here is a way around the expensive cost of bread: Go to a bakery, which usually stocks bread that is only days older than that in a grocery store. Sometimes, you can buy two or three loaves for $1 at a bread store. This may not be as good of a deal as some of you can remember, but it's the best deal on bread that I've seen lately.

Once you stock up on loaves of bread, freeze them. When you're ready for a loaf, take it out of the freezer and thaw it. It tastes almost as fresh as if you just bought it. If you need the loaf to thaw out quickly, you can put a few slices at a time in the microwave for a few seconds.

16:11 Shower Yourself

When going to a restaurant, order water instead of a soft drink. Not only are you being kind to your kidneys, but you are also saving your pocketbook a few extra dollars. Sodas in restaurants can be expensive. At a grocery store, a two-liter bottle on sale can cost anywhere from 89¢ on up, while a soft drink at a restaurant may average $1.25. Refills may be free at the restaurant; but, I calculate that you'd have to drink about seven twelve-ounce soft-drink refills before getting the same value that you'd get at a grocery store.

16:12 Sometimes Eat What You Don't Want

If you almost always eat what you really want and hardly ever eat what you don't want, this could get to be expensive. Sometimes you may not want those leftovers in the refrigerator or that frozen dinner or the can of soup, but go ahead and eat it anyway. If you are like me and could stand to lose a few pounds, by eating what you don't really want, you are less likely to overeat, and over time you are bound to shed some of those unwanted pounds. Most importantly, by eating what you don't really want but already have, you are saving money.

16:13 Keep Sodas and Snacks at Work

Keep an adequate supply of your favorite sodas and snacks in a desk drawer at work for when you crave them. You would save more money by doing this than if you were to purchase these items from a vending machine at work or at a nearby convenience store.

16:14 Limit the Number of Times You Eat Out

Eating at a restaurant is always expensive, so don't make it a common thing to do. Whether it be once a month, once every three months or once every six months, place a limit on the number of times you go out to eat.

Or, limit the number of times you eat out to special occasions only. By doing so, you have just placed yourself on an "eating out" budget and this is one way to immediately cut your expenses.

16:15 Always Eat Half

When you go to a restaurant, make it a habit of eating only half of your entrée. Then, get a "to go" container and take the other half with you. Eat the other half for dinner or lunch the next day. By eating half at a restaurant, you are not only taking in half of the fat grams and calories per meal, but you are also paying for one meal and getting two.

16:16 Share a Meal when Eating Out

To cut costs when eating out with someone, share an entrée, if the restaurant will allow it. Restaurants usually give hearty portions. By sharing an entrée, you may not have extra food to take home, but you may still leave the restaurant with a satisfied appetite.

16:17 Take Your Own Snacks/Drinks

Foods at amusement parks and sporting events are overpriced. Call ahead to determine whether the establishment allows outside food and beverages. If it does, take your own snacks and drinks. If it doesn't, eat a good meal before you go so you won't be as hungry and have to pay for as much overpriced food while there.

16:18 Don't Buy Alcoholic Beverages Out

Purchasing a bottle of liquor from a store costs about the same or slightly more than *one* alcoholic beverage at a bar or restaurant. So, if you must have a drink, do it before you go out; unless, of course, you are driving.

CHAPTER 17

Health and Beauty

17:1 Lose Weight, Not Money

If you were to join a weight-loss center to lose weight, then you would be losing more money than weight, because these centers cost big bucks. Then, on top of the membership fees, some weight-loss centers require you to buy and eat special foods.

When you think about it, foods similar to the weight-loss center's can often be found in your local grocery store, often for half the price. In addition, one of the benefits of joining a weight-loss center is counseling. But, if you ask, a supportive friend or family member might be glad to encourage you to diet and exercise—at no charge.

17:2 Opt for Free Exercise

Instead of joining a gym and paying those high membership costs, consider a no-cost workout. Do fast-pace walking around your neighborhood or on a nearby track at a school. Play tennis at a park with no-cost court use. Ride your bicycle (with a helmet, of course). Elect any free workout over a costly one. By electing to exercise in this manner, you are burning calories and fat grams, but you're not burning your money in the process.

17:3   Don't Buy Stationary Exercise Equipment

Do you know where that stationary bike or treadmill is that you bought a while ago? It's probably in the garage or closet or in an unused room in your house, or you have since gotten rid of it. Chances are slim you are using it. If you still have the equipment, but you are not using it, either start doing so or sell it. Either way, you will get rid of some unnecessary weight.

17:4   Smoking Is Costly

Smoking is not only a risk to your health, but it is also costly to your financial situation. Thus, the easiest advice I can give if you smoke is quit now. If you do, you are not only relieving your body of the poisonous substances contained in tobacco products, but you are also saving money.

Depending on the amount of smoking you do, by quitting, you can save $1,000 or more in tobacco product costs per year. This does not include the extra costs smokers incur to avoid bad breath, and clean smoky clothes and carpet, which go along with smoking. In addition, buying lighters, matches and ashtrays and other smoking supplies is almost as costly as the habit itself.

If you've tried to quit smoking, but haven't been successful, then seek professional help and prescription medication to aid you. Be encouraged: According to one study, it usually takes a smoker more than one attempt to quit before he is actually successful.

17:5   Avoid Expensive Dental Bills

Without insurance, one dental visit can be detrimental to your finances. Most everyone at some time or another in their lives, needs to have dental work performed, and it is usually costly. Even with insurance, the costs can add up. With most insurance plans, you still pay for certain dental procedures, even though your cost may be a percentage of the regular charges.

One way to avoid those expensive costs is to locate a dental school near you and find out if you qualify to receive its services. The costs are considerably cheaper than visiting a private dentist. You will find that the students are supervised and have an ulterior motive (good grades) for performing good work on your teeth.

17:6   A Disability Could Save You Money

If you have a disability, you do have rights. But did you know you also have benefits that may save you money? In many cities, those with physical disabilities and a valid license plate or placard may park at city-operated meters and some airports at no charge. Some city and county property taxes are lowered or eliminated at the primary residence where the disabled individual lives. You may qualify for these and other benefits just by inquiring at the appropriate agencies.

17:7   Beauty: It's Only Skin Deep

Many people pay lots of money to enhance their outward appearance. But unless you are in a profession in which you are paid based on your looks, then there is no need to pay lots of money to achieve perfection. Besides, most people appreciate the more natural look anyway. Coincidentally, it is also the most cost-efficient way to go.

I suggest, to the extent possible, you beautify yourself at home for free. You can shampoo, condition and trim your own hair, and manicure your own nails without having a cosmetology license. More importantly, you can do any of the aforementioned tasks yourself, without doing major or permanent damage to your looks. You may want to go to a cosmetologist or a beauty school (with supervised students) to cut, perm, color or use any other chemicals on your hair if you are not a licensed cosmetologist.

With regard to makeup, unless you are a makeover artist, you don't need a vast collection. Owning only one of each item you use is sufficient for most people. Not only is this smaller collection easier to maintain, but it's also more cost effective.

17:8   You Don't Need Cosmetic Surgery

Cosmetic surgery is expensive no matter what kind you are considering. Health insurance companies usually don't cover it unless there is a medical reason to justify it. Also, anytime you have surgery, there are medical risks involved.

If you are disfigured or a medical condition warrants it, then you may consider surgery. However, if you are just unhappy with your looks and, as a result, you are considering cosmetic surgery, then seek free counseling to help you learn to love yourself and the way you look. It is much cheaper to get counseling than to pay a doctor to cut on you so you can look different.

17:9   Don't Get Body Piercings or Tattoos

Body piercings and tattoos are expensive. By getting either, you are making a lifetime decision because their markings don't just go away overnight if you ever decide you don't want them anymore. It's also costly, and may be painful, to try and have their markings removed from your body.

Before you get a body piercing or tattoo, consider the impact it will have on your ability to get a professional job. Body piercings and tattoos aren't professional, and they won't impress a potential employer. So, by having them, especially if they are in a place on your body that is not usually covered, you may limit your opportunities to work in a professional environment and potentially earn more money.

17:10 Do Your Own Nails

If you've been getting your nails done by a professional, stop doing so. Getting your nails professionally done is not cheap. To get your nails sculptured and to maintain the look, it could cost you about $20 every couple of weeks. Instead of getting sculptured nails, go natural. Then, do your own manicures and pedicures. Or, invite a friend over so you can give each other manicures and pedicures. The money you'd save a month could go toward paying off a debt.

I deserve to be healthy—
physically, emotionally
and financially.

CHAPTER 18

Clothes, Shoes, Jewelry, Etc.

18:1 Is Your Wardrobe Cost Effective?

Determine if your wardrobe includes the basic colors—black, brown, navy blue, beige and white. These colors can go with most anything, and they never go out of style.

In addition, with a pair of black, brown, navy blue and beige or white shoes, you should have enough to go with anything in your closet. Contrary to popular belief, you really don't need fifty pairs of shoes to complement your wardrobe. With good care, both the clothes and shoes you already have should last you for years to come.

18:2 Your Wardrobe Is Not an Investment

Don't spend a lot of money on anything that is not an investment, which is something you put money into in order to realize a future benefit or income. Some people put a lot into their wardrobes by continuously buying clothes. But, the only future benefit you may realize as a result of buying clothes, is a compliment from someone regarding how nice they think you dress. Receiving a compliment is always uplifting, but it will never benefit your financial situation.

18:3   Don't Buy Clothes for a Year

See if you can go one year without buying any clothes or shoes. If you just absolutely know you can't, try six months. The clothes that are already in your closet may not be what you really want to wear, but they do serve their purpose.

My confession: I don't like to shop. So, yes, it's easy for me to save money by not buying clothes and shoes for a year and to tell you to do the same. Sometimes I'll go as long as two years without buying any clothes and, for what it's worth, I still get compliments now and then on how nice I dress.

18:4   Use Creative Ways to Buy Clothing

There are alternatives to shopping for clothing at the mall and paying mall prices. My absolute favorite and cheapest place to find great bargains on clothes and shoes is at garage sales. Another place I like to buy clothes is thrift stores, which offer secondhand clothes and shoes at discount prices. You can find great bargains at garage sales and thrift stores that someone else has already paid the full price for. I also like to shop at pawn shops. I once found a Wilson's three-quarter-length leather coat for $35 at a pawn shop. What a bargain!

Another good place to shop for clothing is consignment shops. At the same time, you may be able to make money by consigning some of your clothes. Check your telephone directory to find a store near you.

An additional alternative to buying clothing at a mall or retail store is to hold a clothes swap meet with some of your friends. Here's how: Invite enough friends to the swap meet to ensure you have a turn out of at least ten participants, which represent a variety of sizes. Ask each participant to bring (from their closets) at least ten outfits and some shoes that are in good condition, but for whatever reason, don't fit or aren't their style. At the swap meet, make your own rules and have fun while swapping clothes. Each participant should leave with at least two "new" outfits.

18:5   Shop for Irregularities or Defects

Clothes with flaws are usually discounted, or you may request that the store manager gives you a discount. Sometimes, you may find that even though the imperfection may be small, the discount isn't.

18:6   Secondhand Clothing Is Cool

Don't go out to the mall or retail stores to buy new clothing. If given the opportunity, gladly accept or buy secondhand clothing for you and your kids. Secondhand clothes sometimes look better than clothes bought brand new. Besides, most kids won't even know the clothes aren't new.

18:7   Buy at the End or Out of Season

Only if you absolutely need to, purchase summer clothes at the end of summer or in the winter, and winter clothes at the end of winter or in the summer, when they go on sale. By purchasing clothes you need at the end or out of season, you can save a bundle.

18:8   Take Them Off

Instead of lounging around in your work or school clothes, take them off as soon as you get home. By doing so, you not only may be able to get an extra wear out of the outfit before you have to clean it, but you are also reducing the amount of wear and tear on your clothes.

18:9   Avoid Costly Dry-cleaning Bills

From now on, make it a point to avoid purchasing clothing with dry-clean only labels, even if the garment is on sale. Since dry cleaning is so costly, you may purchase a nice garment at a less expensive price, but by the time you have repeatedly paid to have the item dry-cleaned, then you have actually spent more money than it may have been worth.

With regard to the clothes you may already have, use a home dry-cleaning product, or try washing delicate garments by hand in Woolite or a similar product. When washing your delicate garments, use the delicate cycle on your washer. Then, allow the garment to air-dry since a dryer can be too harsh. (Caution: Don't try the above techniques with rayon or wool, or on your favorite garments until you have tested your not-so-favorite garments first.)

18:10 Why Buy Loose-Fitting Clothes?

Of course, it's better to maintain your weight. But, if you're like me, and already know your weight fluctuates, then buy loose-fitting clothes. My weight fluctuates by about fifteen pounds, so I buy loose-fitting ones to avoid having to buy more clothes each time my weight changes.

18:11 Wait Before Wearing It

Once you have made a clothing purchase, don't take the price tag off, throw away the receipt and wear it immediately. Instead, let it sit for at least a couple of weeks. This gives you time to decide whether you should have made the purchase. If after a couple of weeks you are not feeling remorseful, then keep it. But, if you are, return it and save the money.

18:12 Diamonds: A Pawn Shop's Best Friend

Surprisingly enough, some pawn shops sell loose diamonds. When you think about it, it makes perfect sense. Both men and women use pawn shops to get rid of their wedding rings (and bands) upon ending a marriage. And it goes without saying that the diamonds for sale at pawn shops usually sell for much less than comparable diamonds at fine jewelry stores.

So, if you're in the market for an engagement ring or a wedding band, or if you're just looking for a nice ring, then go to a pawn shop. When shopping for any item of significant value, I suggest you do your research first. For diamonds, there are basically four aspects—carat weight, cut, clarity and color—that affect cost that you should become familiar with.

With regard to carat weight, the bigger the diamond, the more expensive it is per carat. For example, a one-carat diamond costs more than two half-carat diamonds of the same quality. Also, diamonds are categorized into carat ranges and, from one range to another, the cost per carat changes. For instance, the same quality diamond in a 1.50 to 1.99 carat range costs more per carat than one in a 1.00 to 1.49 range.

Thus, it's more cost effective to buy a diamond that weighs 1.49 carats than one weighing 1.50, although only a .01 carat weight separates the two.

To an average person, the cut of a diamond generally refers to its shape but, to a diamond cutter, there's more to the cut than shape. The following are the various shapes (or cuts): round, heart, emerald, marquise, pear, oval and princess. You can take two same-shaped diamonds and one may sparkle more than the other because of how it is cut. Unless you are a diamond cutter, it may be easier to distinguish between two diamonds based on the amount of sparkle, rather than its cut. Thus, I suggest you simplify this part by picking the shape you like with the amount of sparkle you want.

With regard to clarity, on the highest end of the scale, clarity ranges from IF (in the Donald Trump league), which stands for internally flaw-less, to FL, which stands for flawless. Stones with IF and FL designations have no inclusions (internal imperfections in a diamond) that can be seen even magnified. The range continues with VVS 1 and 2, which represent diamonds with very, very slight inclusions (category 1 has more clarity than category 2) to VS 1 and 2, which represent diamonds with very slight inclusions. Although the VVS and VS categories have inclusions, they are not visible to the naked eye. Diamonds classified as SI 1 and 2 have slight inclusions that are barely visible to the naked eye; and I 1 through 3 (I 3 represents the least amount of clar-ity of all diamonds) have inclusions that can be easily seen with the naked eye. (See "The Clarity Scale," below.)

The Clarity Scale

IF	Internally Flawless
FL	Flawless
VVS 1	Very, Very Slightly Imperfect
VVS 2	Very Slightly Imperfect

(continued on page 124)

The Clarity Scale *(continued from page 123)*

VS 1	Very Slightly Imperfect
VS 2	
SI 1	Slightly Imperfect
SI 2	
I 1	Imperfect
I 2	
I 3	

The color scale (less color means higher quality) for diamonds includes D, E and F, which are colorless (with F being the least colorless of the three); G, H, I and J, which are near colorless, K through M, which are a faint yellow; N through R are very light yellow; S through V are a light yellow; and W through Z are yellow, with Z being the most yellow. While it may be easy to distinguish your preference in size and shape, you have to really examine diamonds carefully to discern color and clarity. (See "The Color Scale," below.)

The Color Scale

D, E, F	Colorless
G ,H, I, J	Near Colorless
K, L, M	Faint Yellow
N, O, P, Q, R	Very Light Yellow
S, T, U, V	Light Yellow
W, X, Y, Z	Yellow

Let me share our story: When my husband and I were contemplating marriage, in addition to doing research on diamonds, we visited several fine jewelry stores so he could get a feel for the type of engagement ring that I liked. While at these stores, we learned firsthand about diamonds from the experts. During this time, we also learned that each diamond varied greatly with regard to color, clarity, number of inclusions, weight, shape, size and so on. We ended up visiting about five fine jewelry stores before we felt comfortable with our knowledge.

Then, we visited several pawn shops that sold loose diamonds before we narrowed our decision down to two diamonds at two different pawn shops. The diamond we ended up selecting was a sparkling round solitaire that was near colorless (G), with a small inclusion slightly visible to the naked eye (SI 1), which weighed 1.76 carats. The one we did not select was a larger solitaire, weighing 1.91 carats. Although it was larger, it was faint yellow (K), sparkled less and the clarity (I 2) didn't look nearly as great as the one we selected. Our new knowledge about diamonds made it easy for us to distinguish the difference and decide between the two. My husband (then fiancé) negotiated to pay $3,500 for the one we liked most. (We had it mounted in a six-prong fourteen-carat gold setting for about $150.)

We knew we had gotten a great deal because while we were at the fine jewelry stores, we compared the costs of similar diamonds. To further confirm this, we took my engagement ring to two jewelers and both appraised it for approximately $12,000. So, the actual cost of my engagement ring was less than one-third of its appraised value. This experience may not have seemed romantic, but it was; probably because we learned about diamonds together, we got the size and quality we wanted for the price we wanted, and it resulted in a great deal.

18:13 Stretch the Life of Your Cologne

An average bottle of cologne can last a while if used sparingly. Know that it is not necessary to put on enough cologne for everyone in the room to know how good you smell. Also, when you make your cologne purchase, make sure you ask for samples. The samples can give you an alternate fragrance when you want to try a different scent. And, if used sparingly, the samples can last for several months.

In addition, you should have a fragrance budget, e.g., no more than $50 a year. You don't have to spend hundreds of dollars to smell good, just as you don't have to spend hundreds of dollars to look good. You can do both, even on a tight budget.

18:14 Jewelry: Keep It Simple

You only need a couple of versatile jewelry items that go with anything in your closet. If you already have these items, then there's no need to buy more jewelry.

I'd rather put my money in a bank, than wear it on my back.

CHAPTER 19

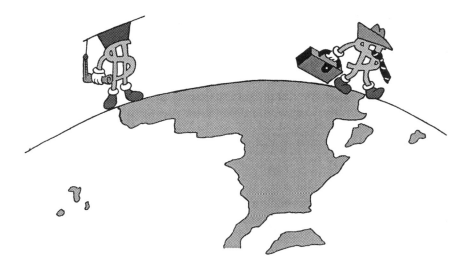

Career

19:1   Get an Education

According to the U.S. Census Bureau, college graduates earn nearly twice as much over a lifetime as non-college graduates. In addition, if a college graduate gets an advanced degree, he can double, or even triple his income.

When you get an education, you are investing in yourself. Now that's what I call a good investment.

19:2   Approaching Student Loans

If you are trying to determine how much student-loan money to accept, the answer is an easy one: as little as you need. Basically, accept the bare minimum to pay for your tuition, books, school supplies and living expenses during your years as a student. Do not accept student loans to buy a car, furnish an apartment, take a trip or for anything else that's not directly school related. Once you've graduated and have to start paying those loans back six months after graduation, you'll be glad you didn't.

If you have already graduated from college and find yourself drowning in student loans, what do you do? Consolidate them if possible, and secure the lowest interest rate you can find on the amount. Make the loans a priority when paying them off because although they are usually funded by lending institutions, many are guaranteed by government entities. Thus, not repaying your student loans could result in federal tax consequences, along with other credit problems.

19:3   Go to School, Especially if Your Company Pays

It's always a good idea to get as much education as you possibly can. However, if your job has a program that provides you full or partial tuition reimbursement and your work schedule would allow you the flexibility, then there's no question that going back to school would benefit you. If you don't know whether your company has such a program, then find out.

If you already know your company doesn't have such a program, then try and convince the appropriate personnel it should. A good argument for implementing such a program could be: the better your education, the more you would benefit the company. The company should want to benefit. So, if the management believes it has something to gain by sending you back to school, your company is more likely to foot the bill.

19:4   When Is It Time to Find Another Job?

As discussed in Section 19:1, the more education you have, the more likely you are to earn a better salary. Also, more education may give you the flexibility to make career changes. Once you have a degree, if you are not earning the salary you think you should be, then it's time to start looking for another job. Specifically, if you know that others with comparable education and experience are earning more, or that your salary growth potential is virtually nonexistent at your current job, then it's time to move on.

Never quit your job until you have another one. Looking for another job when you already have a job is less stressful than looking for one when you are unemployed. Also, even if you don't find one right away, searching for a job can be beneficial because you're testing your marketability and can make any necessary adjustments (e.g., gaining more experience, getting more education or learning a skill) to help you find a better position.

19:5   Do Your Own Résumé

If you or anyone you know has access to a computer, then you can do your own résumé. Just check out a book from the library on how to prepare one, or ask people in your field for a copy of theirs. Get at least three or four samples, then use a format similar to the one that impresses you the most.

19:6   What to Do when You Get a Raise

Don't increase your standard of living each time you get a raise. Put the extra money in an interest-bearing savings account so you can pay off your debts at a much faster pace.

19:7   Look for Free/Cheap Credit Hours

Continuing-education credit hours can be expensive. If you have a professional license that requires you to complete continuing-education credit hours, then look for free or cheap credits.

As a practicing attorney, I receive lots of brochures advertising courses for hundreds of dollars each. Since every year I am required to complete a certain number of continuing legal education credit hours, I find free courses. It's worth it because I save hundreds of dollars each year.

19:8   Start a Home-Based Business

Everyone has something they are good at doing. It's up to you to find out how you can use your talents and creativity to your financial advantage. Determine what it is you love to do so much that you would even be willing to do it for free, and turn it into a home-based business. Making money is easier when people are doing something they really love.

Once you have earned money in your home-based business, track and save all of your net earnings. Remember, you were living okay and paying your bills prior to capitalizing off your home-based business earnings, so you shouldn't need to spend even one dollar of your newfound income until you are ready to pay off a debt.

The major benefits of having a home-based business are the federal tax advantages. The IRS lets you deduct all of your business-related expenses. By saving 100% of your earnings from your home-based business while capitalizing from the tax advantages, and putting all of that extra money in your growing interest-bearing savings account, you are much closer than you think to becoming totally debt-free.

I make money;
money doesn't make me.

CHAPTER 20

Transportation

20:1 A Car Note: Not a Way of Life

Believe it or not, having a car note should not be a way of life. By taking care of the car you have, you can ensure it will last long after you pay it off.

It's understandable that the older your car gets, the more attracted you may become to newer model cars. However, keep in mind that having a car note should be something you look forward to *not* having for years after you have made that final payment on the car you already have.

Wait until you are forced to buy another car. Hopefully, by this time, you would have saved enough money to pay cash for it.

20:2 Find a Less Costly, But Reliable Car

You don't ever need to pay $15,000 to $20,000 or more for a car when there are some good cars for sale that are five or ten years old or older. Some of these cars you can purchase for under $5,000. The newspaper and car auctions are good sources for finding such a vehicle.

20:3   When Car Shopping, Be Prepared

Prior to ever going to a car dealership, do your research. Find out the base cost, the markup, the costs to add extra features and what comparable cars are selling for. So when a suave salesperson tries to convince you he is giving you a good deal, you will know whether he is telling you the truth because you will have done your homework.

20:4   Sell It, Don't Trade It In

You would get more for your car if you would sell it instead of trading it in. Car salespeople want you to pay as much as they can get, but they want to pay you much less than your car is really worth. However, if you sell your car, you could get more for it than the dealership is willing to give you.

Expend a little extra time and energy by putting a "for sale" sign in your car window or putting an advertisement in the local newspaper. By selling your car, you will find that you are likely to get more for it. (Note: Whether you decide to sell your car or trade it in, if you owe more than you can get for it, then you are responsible to the lien holder for the difference.)

20:5   Should You Buy an Extended Warranty?

Ever ask yourself this question, especially after you've purchased an automobile? In fact, a high-pressure car salesperson may convince you to pay for an extended warranty you may not even need, or ever have to use.

Extended warranties usually don't cover what you expect them to. They usually cover parts of the automobile that the manufacturer is betting the odds won't break down within the time frame covered.

Consider putting the money you would have paid for an extended warranty aside and paying for any repairs, if needed, from that account. You may end up ahead financially, unless you've purchased a "lemon" to begin with.

20:6   Buy a Pre-owned Car

Most of us have heard that once you purchase a brand-new car and drive it off the dealership's lot, it depreciates significantly. Well that's actually true. In fact, some reports have indicated that a new car loses more than 50% of its value within the first two years of ownership. So, why not purchase a pre-owned car, which someone else has already incurred this cost for you? Many pre-owned models are very good ones.

I bought my car when it was two years old and had about 40,000 miles on it. After researching the best deal for the cost of a comparable new car, I found I had saved $12,000 by purchasing a pre-owned one. After six years of ownership, my pre-owned car still drives as good as it did the day I bought it.

20:7 Buy the Cloned Version

You can save thousands of dollars if you consider purchasing a cloned, less expensive model. For example, the Infinity I30 sells for thousands more than the Nissan Maxima. The Honda Accord sells for less than the Acura 3.2 TL. The Lexus ES 300 costs considerably more than the Toyota Camry. The Chevrolet Geo Tracker sells for less than the Suzuki Sidekick; and the Geo Prizm, less than the Toyota Corolla. There are many other examples of car clones.

Although sometimes made by the same company in the same factory, the prestigious name of a car can boost its price by sometimes more than $10,000. Having a more expensive or prestigious car is exciting and fun the first two or three months, but it isn't so exciting and fun for the remaining time you have to pay the car note.

20:8 Don't Lease a Car

Leasing a car is just as—and sometimes even more expensive—as buying a car. First, when leasing a car, you may still have to pay a huge down payment and expensive monthly payments toward something you are not going to own. Second, if at the end of the lease you decide to purchase the car, you'll probably end up paying thousands of dollars more than if you had just purchased it to begin with. Third, you're bound to a lease agreement that imposes costly penalties if you default on the terms of the contract.

Fourth, the contract may include mileage limitations. Fifth, at the end of the lease, you are responsible for any repairs to the vehicle above ordinary wear and tear, as determined by the company. Sixth, if you continue to lease, you will be making never-ending car payments just to have transportation.

On the other hand, if you are buying a car, you can one day look forward to owning it free and clear. Many people go years without having a car payment because they keep their cars long after making the final payment. Some of these people have very few car problems. Although it's a fact that if you keep a car for a few years, you will have to replace major parts at some time or another, but it is much cheaper in the long run, than leasing a car.

20:9   Learn to Do Your Own Minor Repairs

Whether you need an oil or filter change, fluids topped off, a jump-start or to fix a flat tire, it would be cheaper if you learn to do these tasks yourself. Even if you have family members and friends you can call on to do these repairs (and maintenance tasks) for free, you still should learn how to do them yourself, just in case relatives are not available when you need them. (Many men may already know how to do these tasks, so ladies, this section is dedicated mainly to you.)

20:10   Dealership Repairs Are a Rip-off

Beware when you take your car into the dealership for repairs: You may pay more than if you were to take your car to a regular automotive repair shop. Recently, I took my car to the dealership for my 120,000-mile service check and the workers told me it would cost $4,200 for this check and to replace some major parts. I then took my car to a regular automotive repair shop and told the mechanic what I needed done. I paid $700 total (parts and labor). Wow, this cost was six times less than what the dealership would have charged me for the same work.

20:11   Buy Your Parts and Pay for Labor Only

Sometimes auto mechanics increase the costs of repairs by charging you more for parts than what they paid. To avoid being overcharged, find a mechanic who will allow you to buy your own parts and charge you only for the labor. Then, go to an auto-supply store and buy the necessary parts. This way, you'll know how much you're paying for your parts and labor.

Some mechanics will not guarantee their work if you bring in your own parts. In such instances, you can shop around for the best price on the parts you need, then allow the mechanic to purchase the parts directly from the store where you have found the best deal. By doing this, you are circumventing the problem of a mechanic not wanting to guarantee his work on parts you brought in if something should go wrong with the installed parts.

20:12 Don't Get "Tired" Out

Beware when you go to buy new tires because if you're not careful, you may get ripped off. Depending on the size tires your vehicle requires, the length of warranty you want, the speed rating you choose and the brand you select, the cost for four tires can range anywhere from $100 to more than $800. Find out the tire size that fits your vehicle before you go shopping. You don't have much flexibility when it comes to the tire size, but when it comes to the brand name, warranty and speed rating, you do have choices, which are a big factor in how much you will end up spending.

Some tire salespeople, like any other salespeople, use their persuasive tactics to get you to purchase well-known, more expensive brands, higher speed ratings and longer warranties. Tires with more expensive brand names don't guarantee better quality. Also, more expensive tires don't necessarily carry longer warranties, and specific speed-rated tires are hardly ever driven at their maximum speed.

I recommend you talk to several tire professionals, especially those with no apparent motive to sell you more expensive tires. Ask them what is the lowest speed rating that could safely be driven on your type of vehicle. Find out which tires are on sale, or which ones are the least expensive. Then, determine which of these offer the greatest mileage warranty. Also, since it is recommended that you get your tires rotated and balanced every several thousand miles, make sure your cost includes free rotation and balance for the life of your tires. By doing your research, you may find a set of good, reliable tires for less.

20:13 Compare Automobile-Rental Rates

Each time you plan to rent a car, before selecting a specific car-rental company, compare rates. Don't assume that if one company gave you a good rate once, it is going to always give you the best rate. Also, don't forget to ask if the car-rental company offers any discounts.

20:14 Understand Your Rental Agreement

Before you drive off the lot, there are certain points you should verify with the car-rental company. After confirming whether you qualify for any discounts, decide if you want an unlimited mileage benefit and, before you leave the lot, verify whether your written rental agreement indicates unlimited mileage. You wouldn't believe how many people make this mistake and don't realize it until they have driven a number of miles.

Also, know the extent of your liability before you waive or accept the coverage. If your automobile insurance policy covers rental cars, then you may want to waive this coverage. Certain major credit cards offer automobile-rental insurance coverage at no additional charge. Find out if you have one that does, but don't get another credit card just for this benefit.

Before you leave, know the exact hour and minute that you must return the car without incurring late charges. Finally, have the car-rental representative insert and initial any verbal changes he makes to the written agreement.

20:15 Don't Drive Around Just for the Heck of It

By driving around with nowhere to go, you are putting unnecessary mileage and wear and tear on your car and you are also paying more money for gasoline. If you just want to get out of the house, go for a walk or for a bicycle ride. It doesn't cost you anything to do so.

20:16 Don't Pay a Traffic Citation Just Yet

As a former prosecutor of traffic violators, I happen to know that there are several possible ways to get out of paying for citations. So, if you are issued a traffic citation, don't pay it just yet because you might be able to escape the fine, which could amount to hundreds of dollars in savings. Here's how:

First, request that your case be set for pretrial. At the pretrial, ask to review your original citation and determine if it is accurate (e.g., there is not a significant error with your name; the street block and name where the alleged violation occurred is correct). If any of these items is incorrect, then file a Motion to Quash the citation. A Motion to Quash is a request that the court throw out the citation because of error(s).

Since the citation usually serves as the complaint, if it is thrown out, then your case is dismissed and can't be prosecuted.

If after reviewing the citation, you determine it is correct, request that your case be set for trial. You can either request a trial by the judge or a trial by a jury. (Note: It doesn't matter which one you request because you shouldn't plan on going through with the trial, and I'll give you the reason why later.) If, on the date and time of your scheduled trial, the police officer who issued you the citation cannot appear in court to testify against you, then your case is dismissed.

However, if your case is dismissed because of the officer's absence, at the discretion of the prosecutor, she may request a Motion for Continuance, asking the court to reset the case because the officer couldn't attend. If the judge grants the motion, it allows the prosecutor to reschedule your case, giving the officer another chance to be present in court for your trial. (In most instances, especially in big cities, judges don't usually grant these types of motions because of the backlog of cases the court already has to hear.)

If the officer does show up, then ask the prosecutor if the officer remembers you. If an officer will admit that he does not remember you being the one whom he stopped for a traffic violation and issued the citation, then here is another opportunity for you to get off the hook. In essence, there is no case if a witness can't identify the alleged violator. However, this rarely happens with an officer who is supposed to be trained to be able to identify people, months and even years later. (Note: Even if he doesn't remember issuing you a citation, an officer normally won't admit it, so don't count on getting a dismissal this way.) But, if this were to happen, it would more likely occur in a big city where officers issue hundreds of traffic citations annually and court dockets to hear cases are so backlogged that your case wouldn't be set for trial until months and maybe even a year after you've been issued the citation.

Further, if your officer shows up, remembers issuing you the citation and the citation is accurate, then the prosecutor will announce "ready for trial." If this happens, then you have several options: You can plea bargain to take a defensive-driving or driver-safety course to keep the traffic violation off your record (if you're in a state that allows you to), and qualify to receive an automobile insurance discount at the same time. You may request that you receive deferred adjudication, which entails paying a fine and receiving probation for a set time. If you successfully complete the probation, the violation never goes on your driving record.

You can negotiate with the prosecutor or judge to reduce your fine, pay the fine or go through with the trial because you've run out of available options.

However, I recommend you not go through with the trial because the odds are stacked against you. I have found that even if you testify under oath that you did not commit the traffic violation, it's nearly impossible to be found not guilty in a traffic violation case when an officer testifies to the contrary, unless you can prove you have a valid defense. One possible defense could be proof of an improperly working or installed traffic device at the time the citation was issued. Also, be advised that claiming ignorance of the law, e.g., you didn't know the speed limit, is not a valid defense for a traffic violation.

Now that you know the general gist of how things may operate, you can follow these steps yourself, without hiring an attorney. Each city may vary with regard to how they do things, so you may need to ask a few questions, but under no circumstances do you need to pay an attorney legal fees to get you through such a simple, straight-forward process.

20:17 Already Paid for Roadside Assistance?

Did you know that *free* roadside assistance is available to you, in case of emergencies, in some major cities along major highways? This service is paid for by tax dollars. The service may include changing a tire, filling a gas tank and jump-starting a car. The Texas Department of Transportation offers this service. So, if you're in Texas, call this department to get the numbers you'd call for emergencies and keep them in your glove compartment.

Whatever state you are in, call its transportation or highway department. Determine if it also offers free (or should I say, already paid for) emergency roadside assistance.

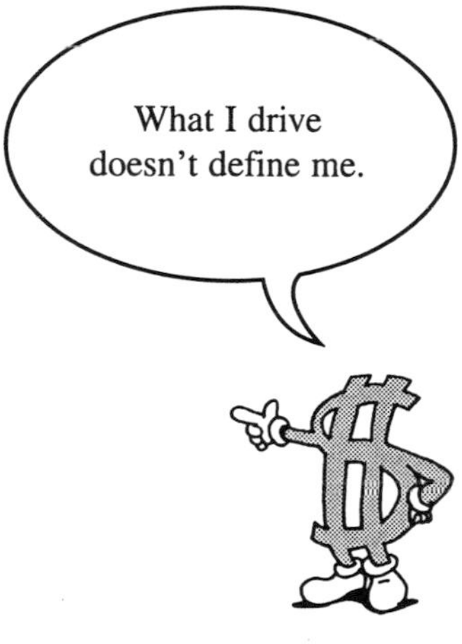
What I drive
doesn't define me.

CHAPTER 21

Relationships

21:1   Frugality and Dating Go Together

If you are dating, then you already know that it can be costly, especially for men who traditionally pay for most of the dates. Well, here are a few tips to help you out:

From the very first date, plan what you are going to do. Since, at this point, you may not know if you will continue to date the person, try to find free or inexpensive activities. But, if there is something you want to do and it involves spending money, determine whether a coupon or discount may be available. If you are paying, don't be ashamed to tell your date that you will be using a coupon. If you are not paying, still bring along a coupon and offer it as a nice gesture to your paying date. Your date should not only respect your frugality, but also appreciate your honesty about your frugality.

Some people you date may end up leaving false impressions of having lots of money or being rich when they are not. So, if you are dating someone who wants to impress you by spending big bucks, explain to him that this doesn't impress you. Or, if you are dating someone who requires you to spend big bucks on him, then explain that spending lots of money on dates is not in your budget. If your date doesn't appreciate your honesty and realize there's more to a good date than spending lots of money, then consider whether this is a person you really want to spend time with.

Dating in and of itself, especially the first date, can be uncomfortable because you may not know the person well and he may not know you. Adding such issues as spending money can make things even more awkward. To lessen the potential for awkwardness, I suggest you and your date establish that paying full price won't make the date a more enjoyable one. It's up to the two of you to make the most of your time.

21:2   Singles/Dating Clubs Are Costly

If you are single and looking for love, you could be searching in the most expensive places if you have considered joining a dating/singles club or service. They play upon a single person's loneliness by advertising their ability to find the perfect mate for you, while taking in big bucks. The memberships are not only costly, but there is no guarantee you will find a person whom you want to date and who wants to date you.

Before giving these clubs your money, consider becoming your own dating service. Start doing things you enjoy, such as traveling, playing sports or joining social organizations that interest you, while focusing your efforts on surrounding yourself with people whose company you enjoy. (Make an effort to keep your activities low in cost.) By doing this, you may find a mate who has some of the same interests as you and only for the cost of the activity. Or, get in some free advertising by telling your friends and relatives that you would like for them to be on the look out for you.

21:3   Prepare a Nuptial Agreement

Recently married or getting married? If so, consider doing a pre- or post-nuptial agreement. Let's hope you will never need it because your marriage will last forever. Realistically these days more than half of all marriages end in divorce. Just in case yours is one of those, then it's better to be safe than sorry.

If you and your spouse or fiancé are both broke and don't have any assets, then you don't need a nuptial agreement. However, if you or your mate is coming into the marriage with assets, real or personal property, your own business, investments, stock, etc., then it's best to prepare an agreement.

This agreement may be prepared before (prenuptial) or after you marry (post-nuptial). Although some people warn against this, it can be prepared without attorneys being involved. (But, if one party is represented by an attorney, the other should be.) All that is required is for you and your mate to fully disclose *all* of your assets, then put on paper which of you is to maintain these assets in the event of a divorce (or death).

The agreement must be considered fair to both parties, i.e., not leave one party destitute, to minimize the chances of being nullified by the courts, if challenged. To encourage equity in long-term marriages, you may state that the agreement terminates after a specified time. Once the two of you have come to an agreement and have put it in writing, then you both must sign (and date) the document in order for it to be valid.

You may find that preparing a nuptial agreement is not the most romantic thing to do, in fact it may be downright uncomfortable for you and your sweetheart. But, once the two of you have completed this agreement, you could save yourselves a lot of headaches and money in the long run.

21:4   Cancel the Lavish Wedding

You don't have to spend thousands of dollars to get married. Cancel the wedding and just have yourself a nice, intimate marriage ceremony. Many people spend as much as twenty thousand dollars or more on a wedding and reception, which usually last eight hours at most. Sometimes, the marriage may last just a little bit longer than that, while the bills you've accrued from having a lavish wedding and reception may last for several years to come.

Also, by having a lavish wedding, this special day is usually filled with stress and nervousness for the bride and groom. Why pay thousands of dollars to have a stress-filled day and to be nervous? I'm sure you are going to get a lot of those days for free.

Instead of spending lots of money on a wedding and reception, do what my husband and I did. We invited a few family members and friends and had a beautiful wedding and reception at my house. (Of course, by having a wedding at home, there are no facility-rental fees.) I designed our invitations and the ceremony program on my home computer. I purchased $10 worth of streamers and wedding bells to decorate the staircase, the living room (where the ceremony was held) and the den/kitchen (where the reception was held). At our reception, we had a three-tiered bride's cake and a two-layered groom's cake topped with chocolate-covered strawberries, along with fruit, vegetable and seafood trays. And my mom made a delicious pineapple-coconut punch.

For the ceremony, I bought a beautiful long ivory dress at an outlet store, discounted to $19.99 because the bottom of the dress was a little dirty and had to be cleaned. I purchased a headband and netting for a couple of dollars at a fabric store and, with the assistance of my aunt who is a seamstress, made my own headpiece and veil. I wore a pair of beige, lace shoes given to me as a gift by my aunt a couple of years earlier. I borrowed a beautiful bridal bouquet from a relative who had recently wed. Although my entire wedding attire cost less than $25, our family members and friends said I looked like a million bucks.

Those present took pictures during the wedding ceremony and the reception. My brother videotaped the ceremony. In addition, my husband and I went to a photographer's studio and had pictures taken there.

The entire wedding, reception and pictures came to a grand total of $225. Even without spending thousands of dollars, it was one of the happiest days of my life.

21:5   Registering for Wedding Gifts?

Time after time, I see couples who are getting married register for gifts that are not practical. For many newlyweds, fine china, crystal or expensive silverware are impractical. If you register for these types of gifts, one plate, fork or glass can cost the gift-giver around $20. Now that's what I call an impractical gift for a couple who may not even have a china cabinet in which to put the fine china, crystal or silverware; let alone a house in which to put a china cabinet. Also, it may take twenty gifts to complete a set of fine china or silverware.

Instead, register at a discount store for complete and practical items you can use that require a single gift-giver. If you want to register for a more practical gift that takes twenty or more people to complete, let the gift be a down payment on a house. For newlyweds who plan to buy a house, a gift registry program will allow gift-givers to give the couple money toward the purchase of a home. Call a mortgage lender to determine if this program is available and, if so, ask for more details on how you can qualify. Registries are also available for honeymoons, cars and other big-ticket items.

21:6   A Breakup Can Be Costly

We all know a relationship breakup can be detrimental to your emotional well-being. But, did you know that a breakup can also hurt your financial condition? If you've ever broken up with anyone, then you know during this time you may not be in a good frame of mind or emotionally sound enough to make good decisions.

So, during and shortly after a breakup, don't make any decisions that may affect your financial situation. Also, don't go shopping. Instead, wait until you feel you have completely recovered emotionally. After that time, you may be in a better frame of mind to make purchase decisions.

21:7   If You Must Divorce, Do It Cheaply

If you are getting a divorce, don't allow it to become a get-rich scheme for some lawyer. By all means, I am not advocating divorce but, in reality, it does happen. However, your divorce does not have to be costly. Of course, it is a given that if you and your spouse could have agreed on some major issues in the first place, then you probably wouldn't be divorcing. But one thing you both must agree on is that you don't want to throw your hard-earned money away by paying divorce lawyers to participate in a messy fight.

It depends on the nature of the breakup as to whether hostility and anger will accompany the divorce. But, regardless of the nature of the breakup or the amount of hostility involved, if the two of you can't sit down together and act reasonably, then you are hurting yourselves and each other, both financially and emotionally. If there is a lot of hostility and anger involved, chances are, you won't be able to agree on anything. If the two of you can't come to an agreement, then many divorce lawyers would be happy to intervene and cash in on your disputes. To avoid this, have a cooling-off period to resolve some of the anger, bitterness and hostility, by doing nothing with regard to your divorce for a few months.

After the cooling-off period, but prior to the divorce being filed, if there are still issues the two of you can't agree on, consider bringing in a neutral party to mediate your disputes and agree to make the mediator's decisions binding. Once you have agreed on all of the issues at hand, you may either hire an attorney to do the paperwork and appear in court to finalize the divorce, or you may do your non-contested divorce yourself. If you need assistance in doing your own divorce, purchase a do-it-yourself kit at an office supply store or go to the library or a bookstore.

21:8   For Singles Only

Budgeting and saving should be easier for you if you are single than if you are married (or a couple) because you are the only one that should be making your financial decisions and controlling your financial destiny. Single people, realize that an extra paycheck doesn't necessarily mean extra money. An extra paycheck usually equates to an extra person (your spouse) having a say as to how, where and when your money is spent. And many times this can create conflicts.

Understand that even though you may be living off one paycheck, it should be easier to control and track where the money goes than if you have two paychecks. Thus, if you are single, take this time to get and keep your finances in order.

When you are about to make a decision regarding marriage, you must analyze whether you and your potential spouse's individual views on money management are different and whether your differences may create conflicts. You must also analyze whether your potential spouse's financial past and present are acceptable to you.

To lessen the likelihood of conflicts, you and your partner should discuss your views on money management before getting married. You must be open and honest with each other for these discussions and effectively convey your views on all money-management issues. This is one possible way to lessen the likelihood of having as many money problems during the marriage.

You should also ask your partner about his past and current financial status. Don't be shy about asking because these are things you need to know before getting married. If you have reason to believe your partner is not being honest with you, or if he just won't answer your questions, investigate him before jumping into a marriage. Request a copy of his credit report, try to find out if he has a checking and savings account, and how much debt he has accrued and the reasons for such debt. Even if you like surprises, you shouldn't want to be surprised about your partner's financial circumstances after the marriage. (Note: You probably should not even consider marrying someone who you believe is not being honest with you, with regard to anything, not just his financial past.)

In addition, if your own financial condition is bad, you must let your partner know. It's not a good idea to find out negative things about each other's financial situations after the marriage when you are applying for joint credit or filing a joint tax return.

Before considering marriage, I suggest you and your partner take the time to complete and thoroughly discuss the following questionnaire, "Assessing Your Financial Compatibility." The rules for the questionnaire are simple and straightforward:

- On a separate sheet of paper, you and your partner independently answer each question, with one- to three-sentence responses.
- Be detailed and thorough.
- Be totally honest and understand that there are no wrong answers (although this questionnaire is not a game where there is a winner and a loser, you and your partner will both lose if either of you is dishonest).
- After you each have completed the questionnaire, discuss your answers, without arguing.
- The goals are to become more aware of each other's financial past and present, and to understand your money-management differences and resolve them.

Assessing Your Financial Compatibility

1. What is your annual income?
2. How much money do you currently have in your checking account?
3. If you have a savings account, how much money do you currently have in it? If you don't have an account, why not?
4. How much total debt do you currently have?
5. What is the amount of each of your debts?
6. For debt that is not self-explanatory, for example, credit-card debt, can you explain what it is attributed to (be specific)? If not, why not?
7. Do you know your partner's annual income? If so, are you okay with it? If you're not okay with your partner's income, why aren't you?
8. Do you plan to have a joint or separate savings account, or both?
9. Do you plan to have a joint or separate checking account, or both?

10. How do you plan to share or divide the household bills and expenses?
11. Where do you plan for the bulk of the money to go after marriage (e.g., a big house, luxury cars, wardrobe, investments, vacations or children's education)?
12. How much money do you plan to save each month?
13. How much money do you plan to invest each month?
14. Do you plan for you or your partner to be the main handler of the money/bills? What is the rationale for your choice?
15. Do you plan to change your earning potential after marriage (e.g., change professions, quit your job or become a full-time student)? If so, explain.
16. Do you think that your partner may hide information about his/her financial past or present from you? If so, why?
17. What should be the maximum your partner can spend without first sharing the information with you?
18. What do you like or dislike about your current financial condition and views on money management? What about your partner's?
19. What would you change/improve about your current financial condition and views on money management? What about your partner's?
20. How is your credit rating: good, fair or bad? Explain.
21. Would you be willing to prepare and sign a prenuptial/post-nuptial agreement if your partner wanted you to?

21:9   For Couples Only

If you are married, then you probably have already experienced conflicts with your spouse regarding money. (If you haven't, then you are either a rarity, or you've only been married for a short time.) So, what do you do if your partner does not share your views regarding money management, and it causes a lot of conflict?

Conflict resolution is difficult on any issue. But, just as you and your spouse have managed to resolve other problems through communication, you must sit down, discuss your differences and attempt to come to some type of an agreement. You must establish budgeting and saving techniques and long- and short-term financial goals that are beneficial to both of you.

You must also establish whether you want to keep your finances separate; or, if not, who should be the main one in charge of the money. (I suggest it be the one who's better at managing money.) If you can't agree, then put both names in a hat and draw for it.

If after countless efforts, you still can't seem to resolve your differences, then you must both be open to seeking professional counseling or going to an outside mediator. Compromising is an essential element. Understand that for a couple's economic stability, as well as a successful relationship, the resolution of money-management issues can't be left to chance.

It is a fact that the main cause of arguments most married couples have usually involve money. It is also a fact that many of those who divorce, do so mainly because of issues involving money. If you haven't taken the steps necessary to resolve your financial conflicts, then do so now, before it's too late.

Complete the "Assessing Your Financial Compatibility" questionnaire that's in Section 21:8, even if you are already married. Answer each question in terms of how you would like for your financial situation with your spouse to be, not how it is currently.

21:10 Don't Plan Expensive Funerals

Recently, I attended a funeral in which the printed program had so many pictures that it looked like a photo album, the casket was a fancy bronze, top-of-the-line one, the cemetery plot contained an engraved steel vault, and the vault had a special key that was given to a family member during the graveside ceremony. This funeral was so elaborate that everyone present had to be impressed. However, to me, the service did not show any more love for the deceased than if they had spent thousands of dollars less.

A funeral is not an occasion for impressing others. The purpose is to pay your last respects (not your last dime) to a loved one who has passed on. Instead of planning an expensive funeral service, show your love daily while the ones you care about are alive and can appreciate it. Then, upon their passing, carry out their wishes, whether it be cremation (which is usually less costly) or a burial service, in the most modest and loving way.

In addition, if you are making your own funeral arrangements, don't include elaborate and expensive wishes. It's already going to be emotionally exhausting to deal with your passing, so don't let it be financially exhausting on your loved ones as well.

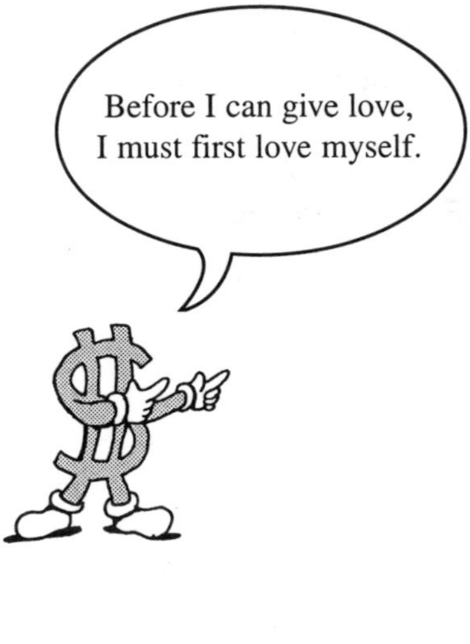
Before I can give love,
I must first love myself.

CHAPTER 22

Children

22:1　It's Never Too Early to Start

Regardless of your child's age, start saving for his college education. This is an important investment because it can make the difference in a person's earning potential over his lifetime. So, start a separate savings account specifically for your child's college education now.

22:2　Paying Too Much for Child Care?

Assess whether you are paying too much for child care. These fees vary depending on the age of the child, the facility's location and level of prestige and the experience of the child-care providers. To determine whether you are currently paying too much, visit at least three child-care facilities. Find out the cost of services for your child's age, all of the benefits the facilities have to offer, the level of education and training of the providers, the child-to-care-provider ratio, the safety and security features, whether the site has a variety of learning and

151

extracurricular activities and any other factors you believe to be important.

Determine whether the benefits at each facility outweigh the costs or whether the only factors attributed to higher costs have to do with such extrinsic factors as the prestige, location or name. Remember, the quality of the child care is the factor you should be assessing. You may find, as a friend of mine did, that a $50-a-week facility located near your home provides services comparable to a $150-a-week prestigious, centrally located facility. The bottom line: Do your research. If you find you are paying too much for child care, then enroll your child in a less expensive facility. Put the difference in cost in an account to start your child's college fund.

22:3   Is Private School More Beneficial?

Could your child be in private school for no good reason? Although many parents may not admit it, some place their children in private school because of the prestige. This is absolutely the wrong reason to enroll your child in private school. There are other parents who place their children in private school because they believe public schools are no good. However, some public schools have just as much to offer as costly private ones.

Before enrolling your child in private school, do your homework. First, check out the public schools to see what they have to offer. Then, compare them with what the private schools are offering. If there isn't a big difference, consider enrolling your child in public school. By not doing so, chances are, you could be paying for benefits you could be receiving for free (or that you've already paid for with your tax dollars).

If after researching, you find that public schools are offering a substandard education, then go talk to the principal or the superintendent about the ways you and your tax dollars can improve the public school's ability to provide a better education for your child. Become active in making your local school better. Before paying big bucks for private school, you may find that a better education in public school is just around the corner.

22:4   Tutor Your Child Yourself

Instead of paying to send your child to those high-cost tutoring centers, consider tutoring him yourself. You will not only save money, but you will have the opportunity to spend quality time with your child.

However, if you know you just don't have the patience to tutor, pay a qualified high school or college student to do it; and find other ways to spend quality time with your child.

22:5 Reward Good Grades to Teach Frugality

Reward your child for her good grades. Once she earns the money, allow her to set her own short- and long-term goals for spending and saving. Then, teach her to save at least half of her "good grade" earnings toward accomplishing those goals, while allowing her to spend the other half on what she wants now. Doing so encourages her to continue to make good grades and it teaches her the importance of budgeting and saving her "good grade" earnings for both short- and long-term goals.

It is important to teach your child good money-management techniques. In doing so, you become the example she should want to follow. This is one lesson she will be able to practice and utilize over her lifetime.

22:6 Assign Chores to Teach Budgeting

Assign chores around the house as a way for your child to earn money. Then, once he has earned it, teach him to budget what he's earned. The important lesson here is not earning, but teaching him how to manage money.

22:7 Just Say No to Your Kids

Whether you are at a department store, grocery store or any other kind of store, say no when your kids see something and want you to buy it. Many companies make it easy for kids—and adults—to fall prey to their advertisements. These companies can count on you to buy their strategically marketed products. The next time you're in this situation, just say no.

22:8 Refuse to Buy It

Don't buy your child designer label clothes or tennis shoes. Her friends may be wearing these trendy items, but it is important for you to instill in your child at an early age that she can't have everything her friends have. It may not matter to her now, but still let her know that the designer labels could increase prices up to 75%. Also, remind her that, contrary to what she may believe, you still love her very, very much, even though you won't buy her everything her little heart desires.

Since kids quickly outgrow clothes, all they really need at one time are five to seven outfits and a couple of pairs of shoes. If they ask why you won't buy them more clothes, let them know that their wardrobe is not an investment. You serve as their number one example.

22:9   Throw Parties at Home

When I was a kid, all of the birthday parties my parents threw for me were at home. Back then, we didn't know about places where parents could host parties for their children. Now, these party places are everywhere, and parents are paying big bucks to use them.

To cut your children's party expenses, throw their birthday parties at home. Your children will have plenty of opportunities to go to those party places when their friends celebrate birthdays.

22:10   Don't Buy Into Character Crazes

Remember Pocahontas, Teenage Mutant Ninja Turtles, Mighty Morphin Power Rangers, Esmarelda, Mulan, Barney, Teletubbies, etc.? After a year or so, these characters are just a thing of the past. But, when they first came out, a craze was born.

The popularity with most of these characters has subsided. But, not before parents spent millions buying their children paraphernalia depicting the latest and newest characters. Don't spend another dollar buying these items. Instead, save that money in an interest-bearing savings account for your children's college education.

22:11   Saving as a Student

Whether your child is in elementary, secondary, college or graduate school, instead of buying her fancy spiraled notebooks, buy notebook paper and reusable plastic folders. Notebook paper is cheap and usually goes on sale right before school starts. Stock up when you find a good sale. If she takes care of the plastic folders, your child can use the same ones every year until she graduates.

Encourage your child to make good grades, not just because you want her to, but because she is more likely to be awarded academic scholarships, which may ease you and your child's financial paths. In selecting a college, encourage your child to apply to and attend state or public colleges. The fees at these schools are much cheaper than those at private schools, and usually the education is just as good.

As a college student, encourage your child to buy used books. At the end of the semester, she can resell them and apply the money toward next semester's books. Also, encourage her to make her lunch instead of eating in the cafeteria. Even after student discounts, making her lunch is still more cost efficient.

In funding your child's college education, accept as few loans as possible, and as many grants and scholarships as you can find. Remember that student loans have to be paid back while the grants and scholarships don't. In addition, don't allow your child to get loans to pay for anything unless it is directly related to her education. Secondhand clothes and shoes, home furnishings—and, if she is lucky enough to have one, a car—should suffice until she is out on her own. She should also carpool and split gasoline expenses with others when traveling.

Inform your child that this is the time in which it is understandable for her to act and live poor. She should work part-time to cover everyday living expenses and needs during the semester, and start early looking for jobs during breaks. Once your child graduates, with no or very few loans to repay, both of you will be glad.

One final note: While your child is in college, strongly urge her not to accept any major credit-card offers. Those companies prey upon college students, most of whom have never had credit, by offering them more credit than they can ever imagine, with outrageous interest rates. Giving a college student her own credit card is like putting a child in a room full of candy and allowing her to eat all she wants. Having access to credit cards is not good for any college student, unless she has proven she is financially responsible.

22:12 Consider the Cost of the Activity

There are just as many free or low-cost activities for your children to do as there are costly ones—you just have to find them. Once you do, your kids can enjoy the fun without the added expense to you.

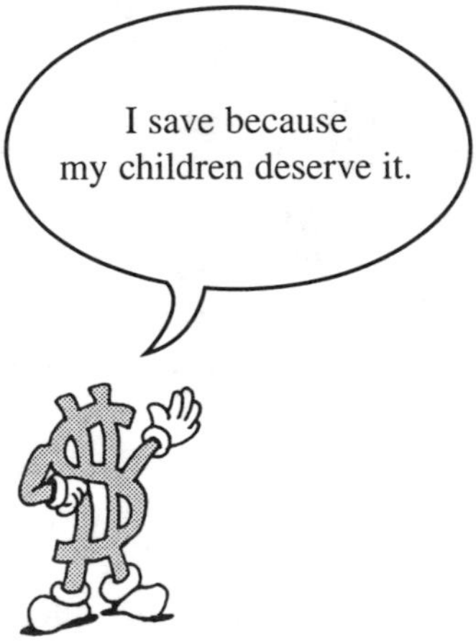
I save because my children deserve it.

CHAPTER 23

Holidays and Special Occasions

23:1   How to Have a Thrifty Holiday

It is important to have a safe holiday, but it is equally important to keep it thrifty. Millions of people go deep in debt each year because they don't control their spending habits during this time of year.

During the holidays, people shop themselves crazy until they forget the real reason they are celebrating. They get so caught up that they not only buy Christmas gifts for others, but for themselves as well. They believe it is acceptable to shop because everyone's doing it.

You don't have to find yourself deep in debt after the holidays. If you are one of those people who year after year, shops herself crazy, then this Christmas, don't repeat the same old cycle. You shouldn't go broke buying expensive gifts for people who are close to you to enjoy the holidays.

Don't risk financial ruin during a time when family, being together, honoring tradition and practicing your religious beliefs should be the only things that really matter. How ever you choose to celebrate, make each and every holiday a thrifty one for you and yours.

23:2   Try Something Different

If you usually exchange gifts with lots of people, explore less costly options. As an alternative, suggest a gift exchange for your family: Place the names of all the adults in a box. Then, each adult should pull a name and anonymously purchase a gift for the person whose name they pulled. Make sure every participant agrees on a minimum and maximum cost for the gift. Your family may want to pool your funds to purchase gifts for the children and cut costs while doing so.

Another option is to reduce the number of people, especially non-family members, who you exchange gifts with every year. You can do this by talking to each person with whom you usually exchange gifts and find out who is okay with not doing so. All who are okay with the idea, you can strike off your list.

A third option that works for my family involves each person buying gifts for everyone from one discount store you all like. My family makes an effort to spend less than $100 total for about ten gifts. Whether you buy a $100 gift or a $10 gift for each family member, your family should realize, like ours has, that showing love toward one another each and every day of the year is what's most important, not spending a lot of money and going broke in the process.

23:3   Buy Gifts that Are Needed

If you do exchange gifts for Christmas, ask the person for whom you are buying the gift, what he needs. Buy only items that are needed. In turn, if you expect to receive a gift from someone, request only items that you need. By doing so, you are saving yourself and others a lot of money because you are purchasing and requesting gifts you'd have to buy anyway.

23:4   Don't Shop After Thanksgiving

From the day after Thanksgiving until Christmas Eve, many people go into a shopping frenzy. It's something about this time that puts some people in more of a spending mode and in more debt than during any other time of the year.

It is best—and sometimes cheaper—to shop for your Christmas gifts throughout the year. By purchasing your gifts during the year, you are less likely to get caught up in a frenzy that puts most people in debt throughout the next year.

23:5   Buy an Artificial Tree

Although live Christmas trees are less expensive in the short run, the costs for them become more expensive over time because you'd have to make this purchase every year. Although the up-front cost is more expensive, buy an artificial Christmas tree, which will last as long as you want to use it.

23:6   Don't Overdecorate for Christmas

Christmas lights and decorations are costly, unless of course you find them where I found mine—at a garage sale. Also, Christmas lights can drive up a utility bill. So if you are trying to save money, don't buy and put up any (or many) Christmas lights or buy a lot of expensive decorations. Instead, drive around the neighborhood and enjoy everyone else's decorations for free.

23:7   Cutting Gift-Wrapping Costs

Gift wrapping can many times be almost as expensive as the gift itself. It used to be that you could get a complimentary box or gift wrapping when you purchased a gift. Not much money, if any, was spent on buying gift boxes and gift-wrapping items. Now, in addition to plain boxes, predecorated ones and decorated gift bags with the name tags attached, are available. Gift wrapping has created its own niche, which accounts for millions of dollars a year. Here are some ideas on how to cut costs:

One suggestion is to collect shoe boxes or any other boxes or gift bags all year long. (Note: You don't have to buy shoes to find shoe boxes.) My family exchanges gifts every year; so, instead of buying gift boxes, we store and use the same boxes and bags each year. In addition, don't buy expensive wrapping paper; instead, use grocery sacks to wrap your gifts. To add color, decorate with colorful strings and bows. Kids may appreciate the use of comic strips to wrap their gifts.

If you must use gift wrap, buy these items for the next year after December 25, when they're on sale for 50% to 75% off the regular price. Whatever you do, don't let a store wrap your gifts unless it's complimentary. Gift wrapping should not cost as much as the gift, unless you've managed to find a gift for under a buck. Besides, the gift wrap is just going to be ripped off anyway, so don't waste your money.

23:8   Greetings Don't Have to Be Costly

Many greeting cards can cost you $1.50 or more per card at a greeting card store. But, why pay that much for greeting cards when you can get them for a whole lot cheaper?

Look for a dollar store in your area, which may sell greeting cards one or two for a dollar. Thus, if you buy ten greeting cards at a dollar store, it may only cost you $5 to $10; whereas, if you buy the same number of cards, even on sale at a greeting card store, you'll pay anywhere from $15 (if you're lucky) to $30. So, whether you purchase one card or ten, don't purchase them at a greeting card store.

You may also choose to buy greeting cards by the box, which is much cheaper than buying individual cards. Another alternative is to write your holiday greetings on your personalized stationery or make cards on your personal computer. Not only will your friends and relatives appreciate your personal touch, but doing this will save you a few dollars. You can use this savings advice whether you are sending a holiday greeting, another special greeting or just to say hello.

Finally, the way I love to greet, which also happens to be the cheapest, is just to say it personally. You really don't need a card written by a stranger to express how you feel. You can do that yourself for free.

23:9   Don't Make a New Year's Resolution

Have you ever made a New Year's Resolution that you didn't keep? If you have, you are not alone. It's just something about a New Year's resolution that people are usually not successful at keeping. Some common resolutions may include improving your financial condition, losing weight, getting in shape or stopping a bad habit.

By February, most people have forgotten their goals. In fact, by mid-January, few people are talking about New Year's resolutions. So, to get serious about improving your financial condition, don't make it your New Year's resolution, one that will be forgotten by the time the excitement and the thrill of the new year is long gone.

23:10 Don't Fall for the Roses

Whether it's Valentines Day or an anniversary, roses are always overpriced. Depending on the time of year, the store and the location of purchase, a dozen roses in a vase can cost anywhere from $50 to $150, plus delivery charges.

There are many other cheaper, practical ways to express romance. For instance, buy your sweetheart something he needs or can use year-round. So that long after Valentine's Day is gone, practical gifts such as cologne and sexy undies, will still be useful. On the other hand, roses, if you're lucky, may last two weeks.

However, if you are a diehard romantic who believes that roses say it best, here's how to save: First, buy your own vase for under $10. Then, buy a dozen roses at a grocery store for under $20. (Many grocery stores have their own floral department with more economical prices than flower shops.) While there, get some decorative baby's breath. Arrange the roses in the vase with the baby's breath and deliver them yourself, if possible. Your sweetheart will appreciate the roses, even if you didn't pay $150 for them.

23:11 Don't Buy a New Outfit for Easter

Going out to buy a new outfit to wear on Easter Sunday is as traditional for many as dying Easter eggs. This year, break that tradition. You and your kids don't need new outfits for Easter Sunday, or any other day for that matter. You can celebrate this occasion by wearing something you already have.

23:12 Cut Halloween Costume Costs

Whether the Halloween costume is for yourself or for your children, you don't need to spend a lot of money to enjoy your festivities. News reports have indicated that millions of dollars are spent each year on Halloween costumes. But realize there are less costly options.

One option is to be creative by dressing up in something you already have at home. For example, if you have some extra sheets in your closet, you can wrap them around yourself, add a belt, makeup and the appropriate hairdo and be an Arabian prince or princess. Or, you could create costumes from clothing your children wore during a school play or sporting event. Another option is to purchase next year's costumes the day after Halloween when they are 50% to 75% off.

I want everything I need,
but I don't need
everything I want.

CHAPTER 24

Because It Makes Sense

24:1   Take Good Care of Your Belongings

Take care of your possessions and teach your children to do the same. By taking care of your belongings, you increase your longevity of having the items and decrease your likelihood of having to pay to replace the same items over and over. Time after time, I have seen others not take care of things (or easily lose their belongings) they have used their hard-earned money to purchase. Your rule should be if you spend your money buying something, then you will take care of it and won't lose it.

24:2   Don't Wait Until the Last Minute

Making a last-minute purchase can cost you. The more time you have to research before you make a purchase decision, the more likely your chances of making an informed, cost-efficient purchase. For example, if you already know your car is on its last leg (or should I say last wheel), and is about to give out any day, then don't wait until it does to begin your car search. A car salesman just loves a desperate, potential buyer with unreliable or no transportation, upon which to apply pressure. Apply this suggestion to any purchase, big or small.

24:3   Don't Be Late

You'd be surprised how much of your hard-earned money goes toward late fees if you delay in paying your monthly debts. Having to pay late fees are a regular habit for some people; for others, they may occasionally be late and have to pay that cost. Whatever the case, whether you have paid ten late fees or one, any amount is too much.

24:4   Request a Waiver on Everything

If the phrase ends with the word *fee,* request that it be waived. There are application fees, filing fees, cancellation fees, late fees, annual fees and maintenance fees. If it's a fee, then it can possibly be waived. It doesn't hurt to ask for a waiver. The worst people can do is say no. If they do say yes and grant your fee-waiver request, then you've saved yourself some money.

24:5   If the Pressure Is High, Don't Buy

Rule of thumb: If the product doesn't sell itself, then don't buy it. In other words, if the product requires a pushy or high-pressure salesperson to get you to buy it, then maybe this is a sign that you don't need it, or that you can find a less expensive one elsewhere.

24:6   Beware of Multilevel Marketing

If you are approached by someone who wants to present something to you, but they won't give you details until a meeting is scheduled, then beware. Nine times out of ten, the presentation will try to convince you to join a network/multilevel marketing program.

The focus is to get you to join, then you get all of your family members and friends to join, then they get people to join and so on. The secondary focus is to sell products to those who join. By joining and buying the products, the average person could end up paying from $300 on up.

These "scams," which may also be referred to as pyramid programs, are organized in such a way that the more people you get into the program, the higher you move up in the pyramid. Although each pyramid program may be slightly different, they all usually include the so-called multi-levels of management. Progressing from one level to the next depends on how many people you get to join and the people you have gotten to join can get to join. In the frenzy of getting people to join, any focus on a product or whether it is a good product, is totally lost.

Those trying to convince you to join the scam believe they will get rich by selling the program. There are people who are making money off the sale of these programs. But, I believe the only people who are making the money are those first few people who created the program.

24:7   Complain if You Must

Don't accept unsatisfactory services or products from any company. Instead, make your dissatisfaction known to a manager. If that place of business values its customers, then by bringing your unsatisfactory experience to its attention, it may give you a discount or probably something free. If the company doesn't, then this is probably its way of letting you know it doesn't really value your business. If you feel this could be the case, then don't patronize that company anymore.

24:8   Borrowing and Lending Money

Don't do it. Specifically, don't ask to borrow money from your friends and relatives. You put them and yourself in an awkward situation when you do. If you have had to do so in the past, change your future by creating an emergency fund, so if a situation in which you need money arises, you won't have to ask anyone for a loan.

In turn, make it a hard-and-fast rule not to lend money. Lending can negatively affect your financial condition, especially when you don't get the money back. Try to let everyone who you anticipate may ask you for a loan know that you don't lend money (or won't anymore), so they won't be tempted to ask.

24:9   Don't Pay Expensive Membership Fees

Don't join organizations or clubs that have high-dollar membership fees. If you have to spend a lot of money to be associated with, or around a specific group of people, then you really don't need to be a part of this group. Instead, find "inexpensive" or "free" people with whom you can associate, or hang around. They are probably more fun to be around anyway.

24:10 Use Caution when Gambling

Gambling is like throwing your money down the drain, so don't do it. However, if you do like to gamble, then you are going to do it anyway, even if I suggest you don't. So, here are some tips to make your gambling experience nondetrimental to your financial condition:

First, before stepping foot into a casino, establish a maximum gambling limit. Even if you really like to gamble, your budget should be no more than $100, unless you have as much money as Michael Jordan or Oprah Winfrey. Second, once you've established a budget, with the exception of money to get back to your destination, don't take more than your budgeted amount with you. Don't take any credit, debit, automated teller machine or any other cards with you that would allow you to have access to more money. Since gambling can be addictive, by having access to additional cash, you are putting yourself in a vulnerable financial situation.

Third, limit your trips to the casino to no more than a couple of times a year. If you believe you are not addicted to gambling, then this should not be hard for you to do. Fourth, before gambling, ask the personnel at the casino where you'll be gambling whether they offer free meals or any other perks if you gamble there. Finally, view your gambling experience as enjoyable, whether you win, lose or break even, and not as something you need to do to make thousands of dollars to get out of debt or to better your financial condition.

24:11 Play the Lottery?

If you think about it, your chances of getting struck by lightning, then hit by a bus, all in the same day, are greater than your chances of winning the lottery. My father has been playing the lottery every week since 1993 and he still hasn't won big. Since he started playing, he has probably played the lottery more than 2,000 times and the most he has won at one time has been $3. In all his years of playing, he has probably spent more than $20,000 purchasing lottery tickets. He could have taken all of the money he spent on lottery tickets over the years and invested it, or saved it in an interest-bearing savings account and bought something he really wanted.

24:12 Adjust Positively to a Financial Change

At some point or another, you are going to have an expense that will end. Car notes and child-care expenses, for example, do not last forever. When you have an expense that ends one month, the next month and every month thereafter, when you would usually pay the expense, put the amount in your savings account.

Time after time, I see situations in which a person has made a final payment toward an expense, but doesn't know where that extra money (the money previously spent on that expense) is going, long after they've made the final payment. Don't do this. Immediately after that expense ends, make a positive adjustment to your changing financial condition by putting all of this extra money into your interest-bearing savings account toward paying off a debt.

24:13 There Are Cheaper Ways to Invest

While saving money toward becoming debt-free, if you want to invest in the stock market, realize there are cheaper ways to do so. First, rather than hiring an investment advisor and paying him a commission to complete the transaction, do your own research: look on the Internet, read the business section of your local newspaper, listen to the radio or watch television programs about investing, read financial books, magazines or newsletters and talk to people who have investment experience. By reading, listening and talking, you can acquire a basic knowledge of the market and how it works. Having acquired some basic knowledge, you will be more prepared to join the millions of people investing in the stock market.

Second, realize that some ways to invest in individual stock/mutual funds are cheaper than others because you don't pay fees. Let's start with the most expensive way to invest: going through a full-service brokerage company whose services may include researching specific companies, providing you with a personal financial advisor or giving you avenues to invest in retirement programs. However, you may not need these costly services or, if you do, you may be able to find a cheaper way to receive them.

Also, when it comes to investing, these companies may not always act in your best interest because they encourage more buying and selling of investment products. The more trades you do, the more they profit. In addition, don't expect to learn anything from them because they have an ulterior motive for not providing you information about investing. If you learned, then you wouldn't need them.

You may also invest through a discount brokerage company, which offers you little or no advice and assumes that you are fully aware of how and what to invest in. This method is less expensive than going through a full-service brokerage company. By doing your own research, you can feel comfortable using this less expensive way to invest.

But, the least expensive method of investing is through what I call a super-discount broker (also called a deep-discount broker). These companies do not offer any services to its clients other than the discounted way of investing via the Internet (or by telephone). Their service is strictly an online one. As with a discount broker, you are on your own as far as your knowledge and research of the stock market. But, after doing your research, you can invest via the Internet through a super-discount broker for less than $10 a trade.

Be aware that with any brokerage company, regardless of whether it's a full-service one or a super-discount one, they require you to open an account to start your investments. However, with the full-service brokerage company, the minimum amount you would need to open an account is considerably more than the amount to open an account with a discount brokerage company. A super-discount company usually allows you to open an account with the least amount.

For someone who is a new investor, you may want to start off in mutual funds because: 1) your money is put in a wide range of stocks, as opposed to individual ones, which provide you a diversification of funds (from stock that is less risky to stock that is more risky), and 2) the mutual funds are managed by a portfolio manager who oversees the performance of the fund and acts in your best financial interest. (The portfolio manager earns a small percentage, usually .75% to 1.5% of the funds total assets.) Having a portfolio manager for your investments could be very beneficial for a new investor.

If you are going to invest in mutual funds, understand that there are two main types: load funds and no-load funds. Load funds are sold through a salesperson who receives a 3% to 8.5% fee for the sale. No-load funds are sold directly from the fund manager and no salesperson (or fee) is involved. Some people may assume that load funds perform better simply because there's a fee attached. But, paying a salesperson a fee to buy that fund does not determine its performance, just as a car salesperson doesn't determine the performance of a car he has sold you. Thus, for an even cheaper way to invest in mutual funds, find no-load funds.

If you want to avoid the fees associated with mutual funds altogether, invest in individual stocks. Richard Gonzalez, who's been investing since 1985 and is the founder and president of his own investment club, suggests that if you are a newcomer to investing, you should limit your risks and diversify. He says you can limit your risks by investing in well-established, financially sound companies (blue-chip stock). He adds, you can diversify by purchasing stocks in several different markets to have a well-balanced portfolio, so if one market is not performing well, it wouldn't affect all your investments. However, he recommends that you not invest in more than ten companies at one time because, if you do, it could be harder to keep track of your investments.

One final point: When considering investing in the stock market, your goals should be to learn as much as you possibly can about how the market works, to conduct your own independent analysis of the market and what to invest in and make your own investment decisions. You'd save money by utilizing the above-mentioned resources to do your own research. You will find that if you took the time to learn the ins and outs of the stock market, then you would have all the confidence you need to make the decisions that are best for you. After all, who has more interest in seeing that your investments succeed than you?

24:14 Prepare a Will

It is important to prepare a will so that in the event of your death, the disposition of your estate is determined by you, not a court of law. Although many people warn against this, preparing your own will is always an option to avoid legal fees. As long as you know and abide by all of the legal requirements, which vary from state to state, you can prepare your own will. In Texas, for example, the legal requirements in order for a will to be valid, are as follows:

• The testator (the person executing the will) must be eighteen years of age or older; or, if the person is under eighteen, he was or had been lawfully married or was then a member of the armed forces in the United States or Maritime Service; and is of sound mind.

- The will must be in writing and signed by the testator, in the presence of at least two witnesses (over the age of fourteen) who sign in the presence of each other and in the presence of the testator. It is important that the testator and the witnesses actually *watch* each other sign. (Note: Texas law requires at least two witnesses, if you are in another state, check the legal requirements regarding the minimum number of witnesses, as well as the minimum age required to execute a valid will.)

In preparing your will, here are some things you should do:

- List all of your possessions and to whom you want them distributed.

- Specify the exact amount you want distributed to each person.

- Name an executor, a person you can trust to carry out the instructions of your will.

- State that the will revokes all previous wills and codicils.

- Include the name of the testator's spouse and living children so if they are left nothing, a court won't presume that it was an oversight.

- As the testator, place your initials at the bottom of every page of your will so there is no question as to whether any pages were added without your knowledge.

- Attach a self-proving affidavit that is signed before a notary, by the testator and the witnesses, so that the testimony of the witnesses is not necessary in the event the will is probated.

- Realize that there could be legal limitations with regard to beneficiaries serving as witnesses. So, to prevent your will from being void, ensure that you have witnesses who are not your beneficiaries.

Also, I suggest that when preparing your own will, you type it so that it can be easily read. However, a handwritten will (more commonly known as a holographic will) is valid in approximately twenty states, as long as all of it is handwritten; and it does not have to be attested by witnesses. Although not required, a holographic will may be self-proved by attaching an affidavit by the testator stating that the document is his last will, that he met the legal requirements to be a testator (stated above) and that he has not revoked the document. I suggest that if you prepare a handwritten will, you prepare a self-proving affidavit.

If you want additional resources to assist you in preparing your will, purchase a do-it-yourself kit, or visit a library or bookstore and find a book that provides you samples of wills and self-proving affidavits. Follow the legal requirements (for your state) and suggestions, as stated above.

24:15 Don't Be So Quick to Retain an Attorney...

Some things you can do yourself. Before paying an attorney a percentage fee to handle a minor personal injury claim, a worker's compensation claim, an appeal for Social Security benefits or anything else, determine whether you can do it yourself. In many cases, if you know your rights, have done your homework, can organize your documentation and feel comfortable negotiating, you can handle your own case.

For example, if you have a minor personal injury claim, e.g., no more than a couple of thousand dollars in medical bills and no long-term resulting conditions, you can negotiate with the insurance adjuster to settle it for an amount you believe your injuries are worth, without paying an attorney one-third or more to do so. In fact, one Dallas attorney says for minor personal injury cases he often recommends to people who call him, to negotiate their own settlements. Further, he suggests that to get the amount you would agree to settle for, put a much higher offer on the table.

If, however, your negotiations are not getting you what you feel your losses are worth, then you might consider retaining an attorney. The threat of having a lawyer involved, who may file a lawsuit, can sometimes facilitate a settlement. Beware that although the attorney cannot guarantee an increase in the outcome, you will still owe him a percentage of your settlement, even if it's no higher than the amount you were able to negotiate.

Also, many people want to hire an attorney after they have filed a worker's compensation claim. However, many state worker's compensation agencies have ombudsmen to assist you with your case by advising you of your rights and worker's compensation laws, providing mediation and assisting you in resolving disputes. Most importantly, their services are free. If you hire an attorney, the fees can be as much as 25% of your benefits. Unless you have been denied worker's compensation benefits or your case involves complicated factors, you probably would not need to retain an attorney.

In addition, even if you have been denied Social Security benefits, you may not need an attorney for this process either. You can gather supporting documents such as your latest medical information and letters from doctors to appeal your own case. Do not be surprised if your claim is denied because statistics show that most people who file are denied benefits at the initial determination and first-appeal stage. Again, unless your case involves complicated factors or is at one of the later appeal stages, you can conduct your own appeal and save the percentage fee (sometimes as much as 25% of your benefits) charged by an attorney.

24:16 Don't Accept Free Trial Offers

Behind every free trial offer is one that is going to cost you. Usually, you have to make a call in order to cancel the offer and not be charged after the trial period. If you don't cancel, then most companies who promote these free offers will automatically charge you.

24:17 Review Your Billing Statements

Each month, before paying a bill, review your statement to ensure you have not been overcharged. Understand that companies are not infallible in their billing. By making it a practice to review your statements, you are more likely to catch errors, and hence, less likely to overpay.

24:18 Become Low-Maintenance

Becoming low-maintenance means you don't have to pay a lot of money to keep up a certain aspect of your life. You can become low-maintenance in almost every facet of your life and, by doing so, you are simplifying your life, and thereby spending less money on a daily basis.

24:19 Purchasing a Computer?

Before you buy a computer and hardware or software for your home or business, assess your needs. Not all of us require the latest, most expensive technology to get the optimum use out of a computer.

Since technology is rapidly changing, last year's computer hardware and software may be considered antiquated for a computer guru. So, where do people dump their out-of-date computers and accessories? Believe it or not, sometimes at thrift stores, garage sales and pawn shops.

I found a laptop that was still under warranty that suited all of my needs at a pawn shop. Coincidentally, one month after my purchase, my hard drive crashed and I had it replaced for free because of the warranty. My computer has worked well ever since and has continued to suit all of my needs thus far.

A less expensive way to purchase a desktop computer is to buy each part separately and build your own if you have a little computer hardware knowledge, or have someone to build it for you. Joe Barnett, an expert who has been building computers for others for five years, says you can purchase a bare-bones computer system (or you may already have one) that usually consists of a motherboard and a central processing unit inside a computer case. If you can find a bare-bones system that already has a CD-ROM drive, a floppy drive and an internal modem, that's even better.

Usually these systems do not come with a CD-ROM or floppy drive, modem, hard drive, memory or fan, so you would buy these parts separately and install them. All that's left are your monitor, keyboard and mouse. (Also, when selecting a printer, consider the cost of its ink cartridge since it is a repeat-purchase item.)

Barnett says, doing it this way, you could have an up-to-date computer for less than half the cost of buying one already put together. (Also, if you purchased the parts separately, you would still receive warranties, but the length of the warranty for each part may vary.)

Another option is to purchase a store-rebuilt (refurbished) computer with the warranty. By purchasing a computer any of these ways, you'll save. I've done the price comparisons, so I already know the savings. Check it out for yourself.

24:20 Find a Free Internet Provider

There are Internet providers that don't cost and then there are ones that do. Let's see, which should you choose? The answer is an easy one. Choose the one that's free, especially if you find that it offers the same services you need as the ones you pay for.

24:21 Should You Really Be a Pet Owner?

For many people, owning a pet gives them companionship. For others, a pet provides a sense of security and protection. Some people have pets, just because. If you are one of those people who owns a pet just because, then consider whether the benefits of owning it outweigh the costs associated with it.

It varies based on breed and the veterinarian used, but one study reveals that the average annual cost of owning a dog is $1,000, and $800 for a cat. These estimates include food and veterinarian visits. If you feel that the benefits of pet ownership do not outweigh the costs, then consider giving your pet to someone who will gladly incur the costs.

24:22 Keep Pet Ownership Low-Maintenance

Here are several ways to own a pet without spending a lot of money:

• If you don't already have a pet, but you are looking for one, go to a pound or shelter where it's cheaper (or free) than buying one at a store or an adoption center. You can also find people who are giving away animals.

• Buy dry food instead of food in a can because dry food is usually cheaper, especially if purchased in larger quantities.

• Groom your pet yourself.

• Instead of taking your animal to a pet hotel when you go on a trip, ask a reliable friend or family member to see after him. Make sure you leave a number where you can be reached and specific instructions regarding care and feeding.

• Because fees can vary greatly from one veterinarian to another, call around to find the most reasonable rate. Clinics are usually cheaper than "private" veterinarian offices.

• Don't buy toys for your pet because, chances are, you can find lots of things for him to play with right at home.

• Provide your pet lots of love and affection, which are free.

By keeping pet care low-maintenance, you will enjoy ownership. You will also benefit by the money you'll save.

24:23 Before Taking Portraits, Research
Portrait studios are not all alike, some charge more for the same quality and quantity of pictures. If you shop around for a bargain, you can get the same portrait packages for less. So, before you say cheese, ask how much.

24:24 Avoid Parties where You're Expected to Buy
Whether it's an art or lingerie show, a Tupperware, cosmetic or crystal party or any other kind of event where you're expected to buy something, don't host or attend one. If you do, chances are, you are going to buy something, not necessarily because you need the item, but because you either feel obligated to support the hostess of the party or because you feel pressured to buy something since others are doing so.

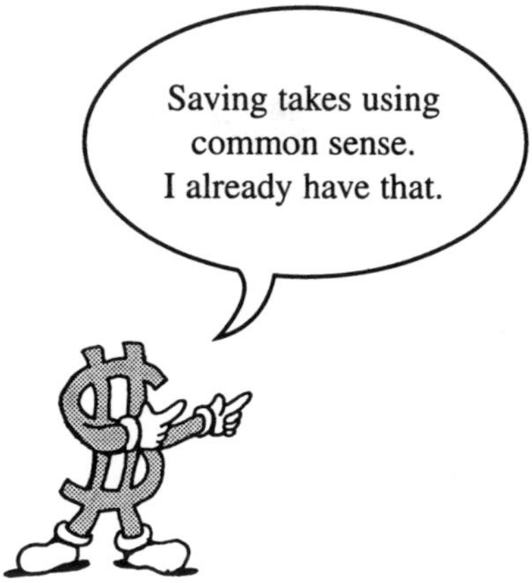
Saving takes using
common sense.
I already have that.

CHAPTER 25

Entertainment

25:1   Find Free Pastimes

As I stated in the overview, most people's pastimes involve spending lots of money, but there are a lot of pastimes that are just as fulfilling and require you to spend little or no money. For five years, I did volunteer work at my church on Saturdays. While others were out shopping, I was doing something I enjoyed that didn't require spending money. Needless to say, I saved a lot during that period. Doing volunteer church work may not be your thing, but just as I did, you can find something you enjoy that doesn't involve spending money.

After my volunteer tenure ended, I managed to find other fulfilling and free pastimes. More recently, I have been enjoying spending most of my free time reading and writing. I also like playing cards, dominos and board games and watching television with family members and friends. That leaves me little time to spend money and a lot of time cherishing hours of quality time with the people I really love—time you can't place a value on.

25:2   Before Paying Full Price for a Book...

Determine its availability at a used-book store, where books can be purchased for less than half of their original costs. All you need to do before purchasing a used book is to make sure it is in a condition that meets your satisfaction.

Another option is to call your local library or bookstore and inquire as to whether it has book sales. If it does, make plans to attend the next one and save. A third option is to determine if your local library has a copy of the book you want to read and, if so, check it out. Why buy the book, or pay full price for it, if you can get it for free, or at least cheap?

25:3   Why Buy the Music?

It just doesn't make sense to spend your money buying music when you can listen to it on the radio for free. Also, you can buy a blank cassette tape and record your favorite song(s) off the radio or from a borrowed compact disc (CD).

Consider this. Even if you do buy the music, you'll either get tired of hearing it, whether you play it over and over or you listen to it on the radio. So, why waste your money on a fad, such as a "hot" song, when it won't even be popular in a few months?

I realize some of you will continue to buy music even if I recommend you don't. If you are one who will, then here are a few suggestions that will still allow you to save money:

• Buy CDs instead of tape cassettes because CDs, if taken good care of, outlast cassettes.

• Buy a CD only if it has at least three songs on it you like.

• Buy used CDs at pawn shops or discount stores where they sometimes sell for less than half their original price.

• Find a store that allows you to trade in CDs toward the purchase of other CDs.

25:4   Don't Pay Full Price for a Movie

Nowadays, you should never have to pay full price when you go to see a movie. Either go see a matinee or pre-purchase movie-theater tickets and save about $3 per ticket.

25:5 Don't Buy the Movie

Buying a video is a waste of money. If you have a need to see a movie over and over, it is more cost effective to rent it and then watch it again and again until you either get tired of watching it, or have memorized the lines, whichever comes first. After you've watched a movie once or twice, and usually that's as many times as you want, the movie may be as useless to you as an empty soda can.

When renting a movie, coordinate your time so you can split a two-evening or longer rental (and cost) with someone else. Although renting a movie isn't that expensive, the cost can really add up if you do it often.

The only time you should consider buying a movie is when you can get a previously viewed one. Sometimes previewed movies cost less than it does to rent one.

25:6 Do You Really Need Cable TV?

Depending on the number of channels you are getting, you are probably paying $50 or more a month for your cable. Say, in a month you watch ten movies or sporting events. You are paying, on the average, $5 per movie or event. That is way too much to be paying, especially when some of the shows on cable television may soon be aired on regular television or you can soon find them at a video-rental store. Unless you live in an area where you can't get the basic channels without cable, reconsider whether you need it.

For the same reasons, buying a satellite dish is also a waste of money, even though the costs of most satellite services are usually incurred up-front. In addition, satellite dishes are inconvenient, they can be complicated to operate and some of the channels are scrambled so you can't even enjoy them unless you pay additional yearly or monthly subscription fees for the services.

25:7 Limit Your Magazine Subscriptions

Subscribing to magazines can be expensive. It costs even more if you buy a magazine off the newsstand or from a store. As an alternative to buying magazines, go over to friends' houses and read their magazines while visiting. Or, ask if you can borrow the magazine to take it home to read, if you promise to bring it back.

Also, magazines are always sitting in the waiting area of doctors' and dentists' offices and hair salons. Take advantage of reading one while you wait. Finally, if you must subscribe, to save money, limit your number of subscriptions to no more than two of your favorite magazines per household.

25:8   Borrow the Newspaper

You may not need to subscribe to the newspaper because every day, already-read newspapers are everywhere. All you have to do is borrow one from a friend or an acquaintance; they may not even want it back. You can save money now if you terminate your newspaper subscription or reduce a daily subscription to a weekend-only one, and make a habit of reading someone else's newspaper when it's available.

25:9   Before Going to an Amusement Park/Sporting Event...

Determine the availability of pre-paid tickets because they are usually less costly than the gate-admission price. In addition, if you are planning to make frequent visits, assess whether getting season tickets will be more cost efficient. Also, read Section 16:17 for how you can save on food. Then, have someone drop you off and pick you up and save $6 or more for parking.

I will do better because I know I can.

CHAPTER 26

Vacation and Travel

26:1   Have Phone, Will Travel

If you are planning a vacation, here is a money-saving tip that has worked for me and my family. Instead of calling a travel agent to plan your trip, call the hotels, airlines and car-rental companies directly and compare prices yourself. Usually, these companies have toll-free numbers, so you don't have to pay for a long-distance call. If you don't know the toll-free telephone number you need, just call toll-free information (800-555-1212), and ask for the number.

Recently, my husband and I were planning a trip to Hawaii. I called several travel agents for price quotes for hotels in the area and I was told it would cost anywhere from $450 to $650 per person, for a five-night stay. These prices were way more than we were willing to pay. So, I found out the names of these hotels, called toll-free information to get their numbers and, with one of the discounts for which I inquired, was able to find a very nice hotel room with a view of the ocean, at $70 per night—not per person—for both my husband and myself.

Our five-night stay came to a grand total of $350 for both of us. Wow, just by serving as my own travel planner, I discovered there is a big difference in the per-night cost of hotel stays, as opposed to the per-person cost.

26:2   Vacation in the Off-season

Many tourist places and cruises have a high season and they have a low season (also referred to as the off-season). During the high season, flights, car rentals and hotels are more expensive. On the other hand, these costs are usually cheaper during the vacation spot's low season. Determine a destination's low season and plan to take a trip during that time.

26:3   Bum a Ride to the Airport

When you are going on a trip for more than a day or two, don't pay to park at the airport. If you drive yourself and park at the airport, the daily cost of parking can add up. Instead, ask someone to drop you off and pick you up. This way, you won't incur any unnecessary parking costs.

26:4   Eagerly Give Up Your Airplane Seat

Airline companies usually overbook flights in anticipation that all passengers may not show up. But, sometimes more people arrive for the flight than expected. If an airline agent is looking for people to give up their seats, be one of the first to give up yours, unless you must get on that flight because you have to meet a stringent deadline.

Airlines usually offer generous flight vouchers for those willing to inconvenience themselves by giving up their seats. Most of the time, the delay is no more than a few hours. However, the greater the inconvenience, the more the airline is willing to offer. By giving up your seat, you can sometimes get a free round-trip ticket.

26:5   Stay with Family or Friends

When planning where to go on your next trip, determine if you can stay with family or friends. By doing so, you save money on hotel costs. Also, while staying with family or friends, they may provide you transportation or your meals, which saves you even more. Make sure, if asked, you return the favor by extending your hospitality.

26:6   Stay at Hotels Away from Attractions

When selecting a place to stay, choose a hotel away from the main attractions. These places are usually cheaper.

26:7   Make Hotel Stays Cost Effective

There are several ways you can be cost effective when you are on a trip and staying at a hotel: One, avoid using room service. Two, don't drink anything from the mini bar in your room. Three, don't make telephone calls from your room unless they are free. Four, take the freebies, e.g., soap, lotion and shampoo, with you when you check out to use when you get home.

26:8   Don't Shop for Souvenirs at Gift Shops

Souvenirs at airport and hotel gift shops are always overpriced because of their convenient location. While on vacation, find a flea market or discount store in which to buy your souvenirs.

26:9   Make Time for Time-share Presentations

When my husband and I go on vacations, especially to any of the islands, we make it a point to sit through at least one time-share presentation per vacation to get the freebies. We have received admissions into all-day, all-inclusive resorts, scuba lessons, jet-skiing, parasailing and dinner cruises.

Although we have never purchased a time share because none has met our budget, we enjoyed the presentations, the all-you-can-eat buffets, the all-you-can-drink beverages and the friendly service. However, with all the perks, beware that the salespeople conducting these time-share presentations are high-pressure individuals who use high-pressure tactics to get you to buy their time shares. These people aren't just giving away free stuff and treating you like royalty for nothing.

So, if you will buy anything that seems great, then *stay away* from these presentations, unless you are seriously planning to buy a time share. The reason is that between the high-pressure sales tactics and the impressive, but expensive time-share packages that are offered, you may come away from these presentations with a time share, but thousands of dollars poorer.

26:10 Use Credit Cards for Reservations Only

Most airlines, car-rental companies and hotels require you to hold and secure your reservations with a major credit card. But when it comes to paying for these travel expenses, pay for them with cash or traveler's checks. This way, you won't get into a habit of charging all of your trip expenses on a credit card, only to come back home and face a lot of debt. Another alternative is to charge your budgeted amount on a credit card and keep the money for the trip in the bank to pay your charged expenditures in full when the bill arrives.

I deserve to be free—
debt-free.

CHAPTER 27

Insurance

27:1   Of Course!

Almost every driver knows about the 10% discount you receive off your automobile insurance if you successfully complete a state-approved defensive-driving course. But, not everyone knows about the 5% discount you could receive, in some states, if you successfully complete a drug-and-alcohol awareness course.

Insurance companies in Texas, for example, are required to give you this discount if you successfully complete the course. In Texas, call the commission on alcohol-and-drug abuse at 800-832-9623; or, if you live in another state, call your comparable commission or insurance board to determine if insurance companies are required to give you a discount if you take the course. If so, sign up.

27:2   Know All Your Car Insurance Discounts

It's time for you to know all of your automobile insurance discounts. Insurance companies whose rates are regulated by the state offer both mandatory and optional automobile insurance discounts. The mandatory discounts in Texas, for example, are for drivers who:

- complete an approved defensive-driving or driver-safety course (six hours)
- complete an approved drug-and-alcohol awareness course (six hours)
- drive vehicles with antitheft devices
- have two or more vehicles on a policy
- drive vehicles with air bags

Optional discounts are based on a driver's:

- age
- annual car mileage
- policy renewal
- vehicle having antilock brakes
- vehicle having daytime running lights
- good grades, if the insured is a student
- away-from-home status, if the insured is in school
- home owner's policy with the same insurance company
- youth group status

Call your insurance company or the state's insurance board to ensure you are receiving all of the discounts for which you may be eligible. If you don't, you could be missing out on some discounts.

27:3   Pay Less for Automobile Insurance

You can cut the amount of your automobile insurance premiums in several ways. First, you can reduce your limits of liability to the minimum amount required by law. Liability coverage pays for the property damage and bodily injury of another, as a result of an automobile accident for which you were legally responsible. Don't pay a higher premium to increase the maximum amount your insurance company is allowed to pay someone else.

Second, you can increase your deductible. The higher it is, the lower your premium.

Third, it may be more cost effective to consider dropping the comprehensive/collision coverage and keeping liability only, for older, less expensive cars that are paid for. Comprehensive coverage insures your vehicle for anything other than collision, such as theft or hail damage. Collision covers the damage to your vehicle if it hits another vehicle or object. You could drop these types of coverage unless the value of your car is more than what you would feel comfortable walking away from in the event of a loss of the vehicle.

In addition, regardless of the age of your vehicle, you could also consider eliminating the personal injury protection (PIP), uninsured/underinsured motorist protection and rental reimbursement. The PIP covers your medical expenses and a predetermined portion of your loss of income as a result of an automobile accident, whether the accident occurred in your car or someone else's. However, you may want to consider dropping this coverage if you have health insurance or another means of getting medical attention and another source of income if you temporarily lost yours.

Uninsured/underinsured motorist coverage protects you against property damage and/or bodily injury if you are involved in an automobile accident and it's the other person's fault, but the other individual either has no liability coverage or not enough to cover your property damage or bodily injury. Because most state laws require you to have automobile coverage in order to register a car, renew a registration, get an inspection and get or renew your driver's license, now more people than ever are likely to have coverage, even if it's just for the short time that it's required. Thus, if you are in an automobile accident and it's the other party's fault, the odds of him having insurance are in your favor.

Rental-reimbursement coverage provides you a specified amount toward the cost to rent a vehicle in the event that yours is being repaired or replaced as a result of an automobile accident. However, if you have another means of transportation, then you may not need this type of coverage.

Before deciding whether to reduce your insurance coverage, call your state's insurance board and ask a representative to explain the different types and levels an insurance company may offer. Determine your needs, then call your insurance agent and ask him to quote you rates. Of course, your insurance agent will more than likely recommend that you have as much insurance as possible, which also results in a higher premium to the company. But, don't let him convince you to have more than you really feel you need.

By limiting your amount of coverage, you could be taking a risk, but assess how small or great that risk is to you. If you feel the risk is small and you are okay with taking it, then reduce the amount of insurance you have and lower your premiums. However, if you are uncomfortable reducing your coverage, then keep the amount you are comfortable with.

27:4   Ask About All Insurance Discounts

Whether it's a home owner, automobile or life insurance policy, discounts on premiums are usually available. Some insurance companies offer a reduced rate if a home owner has safety features added to his home. With regard to life insurance policies, some companies offer lower premiums to non-smokers, and otherwise healthy individuals. If you are not sure what discounts your insurer offers, call, preferably before it's time to renew your policy, to find out what they are and if you are (or can become) eligible for any.

27:5   Shop for Home Owner's Insurance

As previously stated, the elements that may compose a monthly mortgage note are the principal, the interest, the property taxes, the home owner's insurance premium, the mortgage insurance and the amount to cover escrow shortages. If your home owner's insurance premium increases, then this causes your house note to increase, unless you pay it separately. Even if you pay it separately, you don't want to pay a higher premium than you have to. Here is something you can do:

About one month before it's time to renew your home owner's insurance, call at least three different insurance companies and ask for quotes. Make sure the coverage (e.g., amount and type) they are quoting you is similar for each insurance company you call to make it easier to compare. While comparing rates, this is also a good time to understand the type of policy and coverage you have and to make sure you have the right amount and type of coverage for your home.

With regard to the types of policies, there are primarily two. There is the broad form policy that covers everything—the structure and the contents—unless the policy indicates otherwise. There is also the named peril policy, which identifies the specific things that the policy covers.

Under either type of policy, it may be more cost-efficient in some instances to elect replacement-cost coverage for both the structure and the contents than to be insured for the dwelling's market value (which includes land value), and your dwelling or personal property's depreciated cash value. You can choose two different types of replacement cost.

On the dwelling, insurance companies may insure a home for the estimated amount it would cost to rebuild in the event it is destroyed by fire or weather-related causes. (Note: Many policies do not include flood damage, so assess whether you live in an area where the benefit of having this coverage outweighs its cost.) If you elect to insure your home for less than its full-replacement value, however, and the coverage amount is less than a specific percentage, which varies from state to state, be aware that you could end up with a policy that will settle your claim at a depreciated value, versus its replacement value.

To determine the amount of coverage you should have, one agent says he takes into consideration the style, age and square footage of the home, the building costs in the geographical area and whether it's a custom or track home. He says, to further simplify this process, for each geographical area he insures, he has a dollar amount that he multiplies by the square footage of a home, in addition to other factors, to determine insurable value (estimated replacement cost). For example, according to my agent, the homes in my area insure for $60 to $70 per square foot; thus, my 2,200-square-foot home should be covered for no less than $132,000 and no more than $154,000. Based on the geographical area, some homes may be insured for as low as $40 per square foot and others for more than $100 per square foot.

On the contents, you have the option to purchase a replacement endorsement, in which the policy replaces new (of like kind and quality) for old. So, if you purchased a computer a couple of years ago and something were to happen to it, you would get what it costs to replace the computer, not what it's worth now, as would be the case under a depreciated cash value policy. Your policy may also cover your property, e.g., jewelry, even if something were to happen to the items away from home. Keep receipts, take pictures and video tape high-dollar items and put these records in a safe place other than your home. Also, take pictures of your home. If, for example, a fire destroys your home, it wouldn't destroy the evidence of the home's worth and your valuables.

In addition to insuring the dwelling and contents, you have liability coverage under your home owner's policy to protect you if there is an accident on your property or you caused one elsewhere. Regardless of your home's value, at least $300,000 of liability coverage is recommended.

Because a lot of factors may be involved, the agent suggests you call your insurance agent to determine whether your home is over- or under-insured, and adjust accordingly. He also suggests that while you have your agent on the phone, you should discuss whether the type of policy, the coverage and the deductible you have are the most beneficial for you.

27:6   Compare Rates

Every renewal period, review both your automobile and home owner's insurance, then call around for more competitive rates. Who knows, if you shop, you could save!

27:7   Life Insurance: To Protect or Invest?

The main purpose of having life insurance should be to protect your family's financial position in the event of your untimely death. However, over the last few years, insurance companies have developed policies, with much higher premiums, which claim to accumulate cash value while serving as an investment tool for you to borrow against. These policies, which are considered permanent coverage (as long as the premiums are being paid), are referred to as universal or whole life insurance policies.

A universal policy has flexible premiums (within a range of how much you elect to pay) and cash value may accumulate because the premiums are invested in mutual funds. However, the cash value is not guaranteed above the minimum interest rates because it's based on the performance of the investments. If interest rates were to decline from the time you purchased this type of policy, then the policy could lapse and become worthless unless the premiums are increased to cover the death benefit. Thus, the risks associated with this policy could be great.

On the other hand, a whole life policy allows cash value to accumulate because dividends are paid by the insurance company based on the return of its investment of the premiums. The premiums, which stay the same throughout the life of the policy, are higher than for the universal policy because the cash value is guaranteed. Since cash value is based on the performance of the company's investment portfolio, you may not fare any better than if your money was being saved in a money-market account.

There are two types of term policies that accumulate no cash value: the regular term policy and the level term policy. The regular term policy provides coverage for a specified period—usually one year—and premium rates may increase as the policy is renewed as a result of the insured getting older and worldwide mortality rates. The level term policy provides coverage for a specified period of years, usually in five-year increments all the way up to thirty years, and premium rates stay the same over the life of the policy, but they may increase if the policy is renewed.

After listening to a salesperson explain the whole and universal life insurance policies, I decided to keep my level term life insurance policy for a little more than $10 a month for the following reasons: First, after reviewing a chart that showed how much cash value I may (or may not) realize over time, I determined I would rather invest my money in the mutual funds myself or in the stocks of the individual company I choose. Second, I know the benefits of saving and investing my own money, so I didn't want to pay higher life insurance premiums for the company to determine which mutual funds to invest in (for universal life), or for my premiums to be invested in the insurance company for it to make money (for whole life). In fact, I wouldn't tie in my investments with my car or home owner's insurance, so why do it with life insurance?

Third, borrowing against these types of life insurance policies reduces the cash value by the amount borrowed. Fourth, the salesperson's high-pressure sales tactics were a turn-off and indicated to me that he (and the company) had more to gain if I bought one of the more expensive policies. Based on these reasons, I determined that these life insurance policies were not for me.

Before you buy into one of these expensive policies, ask the salesperson to explain the worst-case scenario, i.e., the least amount of cash value you would realize. Assess whether he is reluctant to do so. Beware that these salespeople are trained to use high-pressure sales tactics and to present you only the best-case scenarios. Don't be pressured to buy one of these policies. Gather all the facts. You may find that you would be better off having a level term policy and keeping your investments separate.

27:8   Pay Insurance Premiums in Full

Don't pay your premiums monthly because insurance companies tack on extra service charges if you don't pay in full. If you have a policy that renews every six months, then pay it in full to avoid extra service charges.

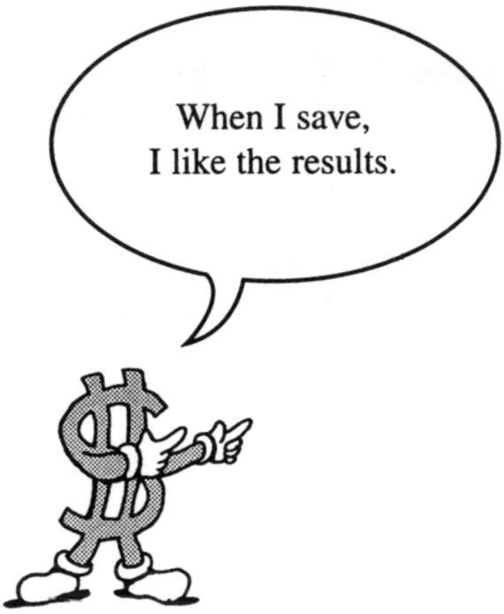
When I save,
I like the results.

CHAPTER 28

Banking

28:1   Direct Deposit Is the Way to Go

Most payroll departments allow you to have your check deposited directly into your checking or savings account. Not only is this convenient, but by using direct deposit, you are earning interest on that money sooner. The reason is that no matter how fast you are, you cannot receive your check, get to the bank and deposit it faster than it takes for direct deposit. If you'd rather put the money in your account personally, then you'd be losing at least one to two days of interest. This could add up to quite a few dollars per year.

Also, with direct deposit, you can allocate your money to go into separate accounts. For example, you can have a fixed amount deposited into savings and the remaining deposited into your checking account to pay your monthly expenses. By doing this, your money is being divided for you without you ever having to lift a finger.

28:2   Find Alternatives to ATM Fees

If you find yourself using the automated teller machine (ATM) and paying $1 or more per transaction, then you need to find another way to get access to your money. To avoid these fees, use only the ATMs at the financial institutions where you do business because there is usually no charge. If your financial institution is not close enough to where you live or work, then consider opening an account at one that is.

Another alternative is to determine how much money you will need between paychecks, and withdraw that amount to avoid ATMs altogether. To do this effectively, you must evaluate your budget. Also, if you go with this alternative, you may want to keep a small emergency fund at home just in case something unexpected comes up.

Some people just love to keep a lot of money on them. Doing this ensures you will spend the money, sometimes just because you have it. Therefore, keep as little money as possible in your possession, but as much as you need.

28:3   Be Careful with a Debit Card

Using a debit card is like writing a check, except it works much faster and is much more convenient. When you use a debit card, the transaction amount is transferred from your account at your financial institution to the merchant's bank account.

However, be aware when using your debit card that you must balance your account as you would if you had written a check. Also, as with ATM fees, some financial institutions have started charging a fee each time you use your debit card. If you begin to incur transaction costs, then it's time to give up the convenience of using the card and either find a debit card with no fees attached or go back to writing checks.

28:4   Avoid Check-Cashing Fees

Time after time, I see people going to check-cashing places to cash pay-roll checks and having to give 1% or more of the check's value for this service. Open a bank or credit union account to avoid paying this percentage.

28:5   Avoid Monthly Banking Fees

Make sure you are aware of the minimum balance you are required to keep in your accounts to avoid paying monthly banking fees. If you don't know the minimum amount, call your financial institution and ask.

28:6   Save in Interest-Bearing Accounts

Ensure your savings is an interest-bearing account paying the highest dividends you can find. At some financial institutions, these are better known as money-market accounts.

28:7   Ignore Enticements for Loans

As soon as you walk through the door of some financial institutions, you are looking at advertisements trying to entice you to get a loan. Don't fall for these advertisements. If you are patient and keep on saving, you won't ever have to think about getting another loan.

I will invest in myself because I love myself.

CHAPTER 29

Taxes

29:1 Know All Your Deductions

Some people prepare their own tax returns, especially if they have no known itemized deductions and they use the simpler forms. However, if you think you may qualify for more deductions than you know about, have your taxes prepared by a professional who should know all of the deductions, which could save you a lot of money.

Below is a partial list of deductions pulled together by accountants at Personal Tax & Bookkeeping Service in Dallas:

- real-estate and personal property taxes
- state income taxes
- mortgage interest
- interest points paid to sell, purchase or refinance a home
- investment interest and expenses relating to investments
- travel expenses relating to managing investments
- fees to collect interest or dividends

- estate taxes and expenses relating to tax planning
- trust administration fees
- home-based business expenses
- expenses in looking for a new job
- work clothes not suitable for normal wear
- union dues
- job-related relocation/moving expenses
- occupational licensing fees
- professional dues and membership fees
- continuing professional education expenses
- portions of your house used for business
- depreciation on equipment used for your job
- some qualified-education expenses
- certain business-related expenses that have not been reimbursed
- legal fees for collecting taxable income or keeping a job
- charitable contributions and mileage associated with charity work
- gambling losses
- some unrecoverable loans
- uninsured/underinsured portions of theft or casualty losses
- travel expenses relating to medical needs
- tax preparation fees
- IRA administration fees
- medical exams required by employer
- impairment-related work expenses
- safe-deposit boxes used to store investments
- subscriptions to professional magazines
- qualified student loan interest
- medical, dental and prescription expenses

In addition to basic medical, dental and prescription expenses, Personal Tax & Bookkeeping Service offers this partial list of related fees that are deductible, but are often overlooked by people preparing their own taxes:

- acupuncture
- air conditioner necessary for allergies or respiratory ailments
- nursing fees
- hospital fees
- contact lenses, including supplies such as saline and enzyme cleaner
- chiropractic services

- medical, dental and long-term care insurance
- hearing aids
- dentures
- guide dog for physically disabled persons
- special equipment installed in home to provide a medical benefit
- cosmetic surgery for deformity relating to a congenital abnormality, accident or disease

By not knowing the deductions for which you may qualify, you could be missing out on money the Internal Revenue Service (IRS) owes you. Don't let the government keep your money.

29:2   Keep Good Records of Deductions

If you anticipate that you will deduct any expenditures when filing your taxes, make sure you plan ahead and keep good records. Get a folder to use for tax-deductible expenses only. Starting January 1 of each year, add documentation and records of all expenditures you have throughout the year that you plan to deduct. The better your record keeping, the less likely you are to overlook some deductions, and the better your tax-saving opportunities.

29:3   Need a Tax Preparer?

If you are looking for someone to prepare your taxes, an accountant at Personal Tax & Bookkeeping Service suggests you beware of the following:

- people who ask to prepare your tax return if they are not in the business of doing so
- tax preparers who will not sign your return
- people who charge you a percentage of your refund
- anyone that guarantees you a refund

29:4   File Early, Don't Pay Later

If you expect a refund, file your taxes early. (If you think you owe the IRS, then file as late as possible, but no later than April 15.) But whatever you do, there is no reason you should pay excessive fees to get a rapid refund when you could file early enough to get your money back sooner.

29:5   Avoid IRS Penalties

Uncle Sam has found a new source of revenue in his penalty assessment programs. Taxpayers could find themselves up against more than 150 different penalties, including non-filing, filing late, late tax payment, underpayment of taxes, filing frivolous returns and so on.

However, the IRS may abate a penalty if you contact its office and show reasonable cause (not due to willful neglect), for not filing or filing late. The IRS decides to reduce or discharge a penalty on a case-by-case basis. Of course, even if the IRS abates your penalty, you will still be liable for taxes due, plus the interest that has accrued since the due date of the taxes.

29:6   Should You Adjust Your Withholding?

Most financial planners will recommend adjusting your withholding amount so you increase your take-home pay, which means you won't get a big refund when you file your tax return. The planners' rationale is that you could be earning interest on the extra take-home pay by saving and investing that money throughout the year.

However, this assumption does not work for everyone. For some, the greater their take-home pay, the more they spend. But, these same people may positively react to a big tax-refund check by starting a savings account, depositing it or paying off a debt. On the other hand, others may actually be able to save and invest the extra take-home pay, but are more likely to blow a big tax refund.

Decide which option is best for you. Then adjust your withholding accordingly.

29:7   What to Do with a Tax Refund

Deposit tax refunds into your savings account. Since this may be the only time of year you receive a big check, deposit it so that the big jump in your account can motivate you to keep saving.

So many people I know use refund checks for immediate gratification. Even if you already have a nice, cushy savings account, it can't hurt to keep adding to it. Then, when you've accumulated enough money to pay off one or more of your big debts, do so.

CHAPTER 30

Your Future

30:1   Plan for Retirement, It's Essential

Whether you plan to go fishing every day, travel around the world or enjoy your grandchildren upon retirement, one thing is evident: You will need money, even if you are totally debt-free. With Social Security benefits not being a sure thing anymore, you must have your own plan for income once you retire. Thus, in conjunction with working toward becoming debt-free, you should be planning for your retirement. Here's how:

If you haven't done so already, join the retirement plan through your job, e.g., 401(k), pension or thrift savings, and fund it to the maximum extent allowed. The benefits include: 1) your contribution to the retirement plan is tax-deferred, meaning you don't pay on that money until you withdraw it, at which time you'll probably be in a lower tax bracket, 2) some companies and agencies match a portion or all of your contribution to your retirement plan and 3) your money, in addition to the matching contributions, is being invested and earning interest so that in the long run, you'll have more money for retirement than if you had just saved for it in an interest-bearing savings account.

If you're self-employed, your company doesn't have a retirement plan or you're already in the company's retirement plan, but you want to invest in an additional plan, then consider an individual retirement account (IRA). Even if you are already contributing to a retirement plan through your job, you may qualify to invest a maximum of $2,000 per year in an IRA. The two most popular IRAs are the traditional IRA and the Roth IRA. Which should you choose? Well, let's compare:

With the traditional IRA, although your investment is tax deductible, withdrawals after age $59\frac{1}{2}$ are tax-deferred, meaning you pay taxes on the money based on the income tax bracket you are in at that time. However, if you withdraw the funds before age $59\frac{1}{2}$, then you not only pay income taxes on the money, but you pay a penalty for an early withdrawal, unless it is to cover first-time home-buyer or educational expenses.

On the other hand, with a Roth IRA, your investment money is not tax deductible, but withdrawals after age $59\frac{1}{2}$ are tax-free, meaning you pay no taxes on the money. In addition, withdrawals made before age $59\frac{1}{2}$ may also be tax-free and penalty-free if you become disabled or to pay first-time home-buyer expenses; or penalty-free, but not tax-free, if you use the money for educational expenses. Based upon these comparisons, I would choose a Roth IRA over a traditional one because a tax-free benefit is better than a tax-deferred one.

Whatever method you choose to plan for your retirement, the most important thing is that you do it—and start immediately. Many people make the mistake of not planning until a few years before they retire, if at all. Even though for some, retirement seems a lifetime away, understand that the earlier you plan for it, the more money you will have when it arrives. Because some expenses don't go away after you retire (even if you are debt-free), you will have peace of mind if you have a sufficient income from your retirement investments to live on, and the more fulfilling your retirement years will be.

30:2   Leaving a Job?

What you should do about your retirement account when you leave a job before you have met the qualifying age to retire (which varies by employer) is an important financial decision. Starting with the most beneficial, here are some possible options:

- *Leave it there, if you are allowed.* (Some employers have minimum account and time restrictions.) Determine what age your employer will allow you to withdraw it without paying penalties or taxes. If you have borrowed against the funds, find out when you must pay it back without being penalized or taxed.

- *Roll it into your new employer's plan.* Check into whether your new employer offers matching contributions. An IRA does not.

- *Roll it into an IRA.* Have your former employer transfer the money directly into the IRA (not to you), so you won't incur penalties or taxes.

- *Withdraw it.* You pay both taxes and early-withdrawal penalties on it, which could be very costly.

30:3   Continue to Save, Save, Save

In addition to contributing to your retirement plan, continue to save. By practicing good money-saving techniques now, by the time you are ready to retire, you will have mastered the art of cutting costs and saving money. The more knowledgeable you are about doing both, the better your life will be, now and in the future.

I am doing a good job of achieving my financial goals.

THE FINALE

I hope this book helps you as much as the implementation of the techniques have helped me to become totally debt-free. As I stated in the overview, money does not buy you happiness, but being financially secure does give you some sense of freedom and the flexibility to find the happiness you deserve. Only you can make this happen.

While implementing these techniques, forget what others may think of you. They may laugh, call you names or even admire you. But it shouldn't matter what others think or say, as long as you have financial goals and you are taking the necessary steps to reach them.

Some of you may think that if you implement these techniques, you can't fully enjoy the fruits of your labor. This is far from true. If you implement these techniques, you will have more fruits of your labor to enjoy.

As soon as you realize it is a wonderful thing to pay off your credit-card debts, car loan and mortgage to become totally debt-free, you will wholeheartedly begin to improve your life. But, remember, whether you live every day of your life deep in debt or debt-free, the choice is yours. Make the right one. Good luck!

•••

To assist you in beginning your journey to become debt-free, I have provided the following worksheets for you to complete and to begin implementing. However, they won't help you if you are not honest with yourself, you don't complete them and you don't put them to use.

THE ACTIVITY, THE SAVINGS

(Month _____ , Year _____)

This worksheet is for you to record the activities you will begin implementing and the projected amount of money you will save by using specific money-saving techniques. The activities can be ones from this book, ones you create or a combination of both. Also, record the specific section, if applicable, in which the money-saving idea is discussed so you can review that section for inspiration and motivation, as needed. Then, at the end of each month, record your actual savings for each activity. Finally, record the total amount you've actually saved for the month. Put all savings in your money-market account until you have enough to pay off a debt.

Each month, add new techniques. Feel free to use additional sheets of paper because you should be using as many money-saving methods as you can.

Activity You Will Begin Implementing	Projected Savings	Section (if applicable)	Actual Savings
_____	_____	_____	_____
_____	_____	_____	_____
_____	_____	_____	_____
_____	_____	_____	_____
_____	_____	_____	_____
_____	_____	_____	_____
_____	_____	_____	_____

Total Amount Saved for the Month: _____

ACCOMPLISHING YOUR GOALS
ONE DEBT AT A TIME

List each of the major debts you want to eliminate. Start with the least amount you owe, or list them in the order in which you want to pay them off. Then, list the amount you will need to pay off each debt. Next, state the date by which you wish to pay off each one. (Please be realistic in setting your dates.) Then, start paying them off one by one.

Once you have completed your goal of paying off the first debt, give yourself a checkmark and begin tackling the next one. You will probably find that paying off one debt will motivate you to pay off the next one.

Debt You Want to Pay Off	Amount You Need for Payoff	Date It Is to Be Paid Off	Check When Completed (hooray for you!)
_____	_____	_____	☐
_____	_____	_____	☐
_____	_____	_____	☐
_____	_____	_____	☐
_____	_____	_____	☐
_____	_____	_____	☐
_____	_____	_____	☐
_____	_____	_____	☐
_____	_____	_____	☐

WHAT ARE YOU SAVING FOR?

In addition to paying off all your debts, you may have additional financial goals, such as building a cash reserve; putting extra money away for retirement; funding your children's college education; paying cash for your next house, car or vacation, etc. This worksheet is to help you identify your goals, determine how much you will need to accomplish each one, assess the amount of time you will need to complete each goal and calculate the amount you will need to save per year to accomplish your goals.

By completing this worksheet, you have just come up with *your* plan of action. Now, all you have to do is follow through.

Goal	Total to Save		Number of Years to Save		Amount to Save (Per Year)
_____	_____	÷	_____	=	_____
_____	_____	÷	_____	=	_____
_____	_____	÷	_____	=	_____
_____	_____	÷	_____	=	_____
_____	_____	÷	_____	=	_____
_____	_____	÷	_____	=	_____
_____	_____	÷	_____	=	_____
_____	_____	÷	_____	=	_____
_____	_____	÷	_____	=	_____

CREATE A PERSONALIZED TOP TEN DO'S AND DON'TS LIST

Make your own list of the good money-management ideas you will start implementing (on the Do's side) and the not-so-good habits you will stop (on the Don'ts side). Keep this list on the refrigerator or somewhere that will remind you, on a regular basis, of your do's and don'ts.

Do's	Don'ts
1. _____	1. _____
2. _____	2. _____
3. _____	3. _____
4. _____	4. _____
5. _____	5. _____
6. _____	6. _____
7. _____	7. _____
8. _____	8. _____
9. _____	9. _____
10. _____	10. _____

WHAT DOES *DEBT-FREE* MEAN TO YOU?

In the overview, you learned what being debt-free means to me. Specifically, it could mean having the flexibility and the opportunity to retire early, take a break from working altogether, spend less time working and more time with your family, spend more time doing what you enjoy, move from a high-stressed job to a less-stressed environment, quit your job to start your own business, work part-time instead of full-time, become a stay-at-home parent or go from a two-income to a one-income family.

Now, here is *your* opportunity to write what being debt-free is going to mean to you. Once you have written down your thoughts, review them periodically. Keeping those positive thoughts in your mind is a good way to stay focused so you will accomplish your financial goals and ultimately become totally debt-free.

Once I become debt-free, I'm going to...

_____

_____

_____

_____

_____

_____

_____

_____

_____

BIBLIOGRAPHICAL REFERENCES

Daily, Frederick W. (1999–Fifth Ed.) *Stand Up to the IRS,* Nolo.com, ISBN: 0873375009.

Eilers, Terry (1997), *How to Buy the Home You Want, for the Best Price, in Any Market: From a Real Estate Insider Who Knows All the Tricks,* Hyperion, ISBN: 0786882255.

Haman, Edward A. (1997), *How to File Your Own Divorce: With Forms (Self-Help Law Kit with Forms),* Sourcebooks, Inc., ISBN: 1570712247.

Haman, Edward A. (1997–Second Ed.), *How to Write Your Own Premarital Agreement,* Sourcebooks, Inc., ISBN: 1570713448.

Hasenau, J. James (1992–Fourth Ed.), *Build Your Own Home: A Guide for Subcontracting the Easy Way, a System to Save Time and Money,* Holland House, ISBN: 0913042196.

Hunt, Mary (1997), *Tiptionary,* Broadman & Holman Publishers, ISBN: 0805401474.

Leonard, Robin (1998), *Bankruptcy: Is It the Right Solution to Your Debt Problems?,* Nolo.com, ISBN: 0873374495.

Matlins, Antoinette (1998–Fourth Ed.), *Jewelry & Gems: The Buying Guide, How to Buy Diamonds, Pearls, Colored Gemstones, Gold & Jewelry with Confidence and Knowledge,* Gemstone Press, ISBN: 0943763223.

Naylor, W. Patrick (1997), *10 Steps to Financial Success,* John Wiley & Sons, Inc., ISBN: 0471175331.

Orman, Suze (1997), *The 9 Steps to Financial Freedom: Practical and Spiritual Steps So You Can Stop Worrying,* Crown Publishing Group, ISBN: 0517707918.

O'Shaughnessy, Lynn (1999), *The Unofficial Guide to Investing,* Macmillan, ISBN: 0028624580.

Parrish, Darrell (1997–Third Ed.), *Used Cars: How to Buy One,* Book Express, ISBN: 0961232269.

Pond, Jonathon D. (1992), *1001 Ways to Cut Your Expenses,* Dell Books, ISBN: 0440504953.

Robbins, Michael (1999), *Smart Guide to Planning for Retirement,* John Wiley & Sons, Inc., ISBN: 0471353590.

Roberts, Ralph (1999), *Sell It Yourself: Sell Your Home Faster and for More Money Without Using a Broker,* Adams Media Corporation, ISBN: 1580622046.

Rye, David E. (1999), *1001 Ways to Save, Grow, and Invest Your Money,* Career Press, Inc., ISBN: 1564144046.

Sitarz, Daniel (1994–Fourth Ed.), *Prepare Your Own Will: The National Will Kit,* Nova Publishing Company, ISBN: 0935755128.

Spiegel, Robert (2000), *The Shoestring Entrepreneur's Guide to the Best Home-Based Business,* St. Martin's Press, Inc., ISBN: 0312242832.

Stephens, Brooke (1996), *Talking Dollars and Making Sense: A Wealth-Building Guide for African Americans,* McGraw-Hill, ISBN: 0070613893.

Wilson, Ray (1998), *Bought, Not Sold: Single Agency, Buyers' Brokers, Flat Fees, and the Consumer Revolution in Real Estate,* Cogna Books, ISBN: 0966013506.

Glossary

Adjustable Rate Mortgage: a property debt in which the interest charges may increase or decrease throughout the term of the loan, depending on current rates; as compared to a fixed-rate mortgage in which the interest rate stays the same throughout the term of the loan.

Agent: one who acts on behalf of another.

Amortization Rate: the amount in which the principal of a loan is reduced by making installment payments.

Appraisal: an opinion or estimate of the value of something, as in property.

Appreciation: to increase in price or value.

Arrearages: overdue debt payments.

Asset: something of value.

Bankruptcy: a federal proceeding that gives a person the opportunity to relieve himself of his debts. Consumers may file either Chapter Seven or Chapter Thirteen bankruptcy.

Blind Appraisal: an estimate of the value of property in which there are no external factors to potentially influence the results.

Blue-chip Stock: a certificate of ownership in a well-established, financially sound company.

Builder's Risk Policy: insurance purchased to cover the loss or damage of a structure during the building process.

Buyer's Agent: a person who is hired to represent the purchaser's interest in a real-estate transaction.

Cash Reserve: money saved in a manner in which it is easily converted to cash.

Cash Value: the actual amount of money that a life insurance policy is worth, which can be borrowed against by the insured.

Cheapskate: a person who carefully plans the use of money to minimize (or eliminate) debt and maximize the quality of life; not necessarily a stingy person.

Closing Costs/Fees: the amount due by a buyer and/or seller to consummate a real-estate transaction.

Codicil: a supplement to a prior existing will, by adding, subtracting, restricting, expanding or modifying the will.

Collateral: property pledged by a borrower to secure repayment of a loan.

Collision Coverage: guarantees repairs when the insured automobile hits another vehicle or an object.

Commission: a fee, usually a percentage of a sale, paid to a real-estate broker for facilitating a real-estate transaction. Commissions are also paid to investment advisors who assist their clients in the purchase or sale of investment products.

Comprehensive Coverage: applies to both direct and accidental losses to the insured automobile (e.g., theft or hail), including equipment, but excluding losses that occurred as a result of collision. This type of coverage is also referred to as other-than-collision coverage.

Consolidate: to bring together or make as one, as in debts.

Construction Loan: money borrowed to purchase materials, pay for labor costs and anything else associated with the building of a structure.

Contingency Clause: a provision in a contract that depends upon the occurrence of a specific, but uncertain event.

Debt: money owed; or, an obligation to pay another.

Depreciation: to lessen in value.

Discount Brokerage Company: an entity that offers its clients very little advice, if any, other than providing a discounted way of buying and selling investment products.

Diversification: the distribution of investments among different types of securities so as to minimize risk.

Dividends: a share of profits paid to account holders, stockholders or policy-holders.

Earnest Money: pertaining to real estate, it's a dollar amount a buyer provides to an escrow agent to show his sincere intention to fulfill the terms of a contract; not required to have a valid contract.

Equity: a home owner's monetary interest in a property after all liens and other charges against the property have been paid.

Escrow: money held by a third party until the conditions of a contract are completed or disbursement of funds is determined appropriate.

Full-Service Brokerage Company: an entity that provides its clients a wide range of benefits including assisting them with buying and selling investment products. This type of company usually requires its clients to open an investment account with more money and charges higher fees to invest, as opposed to discount brokerage and super-discount brokerage companies.

General Contractor: a person who hires others to build, remodel or repair a structure and coordinates the process.

Gross Annual Income: the amount earned in a year before taxes and other deductions are taken out.

Holographic Will: a document instructing the disposition of one's property after death that is entirely in the testator's handwriting; valid in some states.

Home Warranty: a policy that assures the buyer of mechanical, plumbing or electrical repairs for his property for a specified period.

Homestead Exemption: a privilege provided by taxing authorities that allows home owners to pay a reduced taxable amount on a home that is their primary residence.

Inclusion: a visible flaw in a diamond that affects its clarity.

Individual Retirement Account (IRA): a fund established to save for retirement, which is accompanied by tax advantages. The two most popular IRAs are the traditional IRA and the Roth IRA.

Investment Advisor: a person paid a commission to assist clients in the buying or selling of investment products. Also called an investment broker.

Level Term Life Insurance Policy: a written contract that provides coverage for a specified period, usually in five-year increments; the premium rates stay the same over the life of the policy and may increase if the policy is renewed. This type of policy accumulates no cash value.

Liability Coverage: pays for the property damage and bodily injury of another, for which a covered person is legally responsible due to an automobile accident.

Lien: a legal claim on another's property as security for the payment of a debt.

Listing Agent: a person who is hired to sell property for another. May also be referred to as a seller's agent.

Load Fund: a type of mutual fund that is accompanied by a sales fee when sold; as opposed to a *no-load fund*, which has no sales fee involved.

Market Analysis: a study of the average amount that comparable homes have been selling for in a neighborhood or area over a specified period; used to assist in determining the appraised value of a particular home in that neighborhood or area.

Mortality Rate: the frequency in the number of deaths (by age categories) in proportion to the population, used by life insurance companies to determine premium rates.

Mortgage: a property debt; or, the pledging of property to a creditor as security for the repayment of a debt.

Mortgage Insurance: protects a lender against a loss in the event a borrower defaults on a loan. Although the borrower pays the premium, mortgage insurance is of no benefit to the borrower.

Mortgage Loan: money borrowed to purchase property. Repayment of a traditional mortgage loan may be structured in such a way that, in addition to the principal and interest, installments of the taxes, home owner's insurance and mortgage insurance may be included in the loan payments.

Mortgagee: one who incurs a property debt.

Mortgagor: one who deeds property to another as security for a loan.

Motion for Continuance: an application to the court requesting it postpone a pending action.

Motion to Quash: an application to the court requesting an order to overthrow a decision or vacate a matter (to be) presented to the court.

Multilevel Marketing: a method of selling products directly to customers and soliciting them to do the same. May also be referred to as network marketing and pyramid schemes.

Mutual Fund: a pool of investments used to purchase a large portfolio of securities that is managed by a professional advisor. When you purchase a share in a mutual fund, you are buying portions of the securities in that portfolio, creating a diversification of your investment.

Net Income: the amount earned after taxes and other deductions are removed.

Nuptial Agreement: an arrangement pertaining to marriage.

Ombudsmen: government officials who help resolve disputes.

Origination Fee: a one-time fee, usually 1% of the loan amount, charged by a mortgage lender at the time a loan is funded.

Personal Injury Protection: insurance coverage for medical expenses and a predetermined portion of loss of income, as a result of a person being in an automobile accident.

Point: one percent of the loan amount purchased by a mortgagee to reduce the interest rate on the loan. Each point equals one percent. Mortgage lenders usually allow the purchase of up to three points.

Portfolio Manager: a professional who governs the investments of others. Also called a fund manager.

Post-nuptial Agreement: a contract entered into by a husband and wife to determine the rights of each spouse in the other's property in the event of death or divorce.

Prenuptial Agreement: a contract entered into by two people who intend to marry, which sets forth the rights of each person in the other's property in the event of divorce or death.

Principal: the buyer or seller in a real-estate transaction; or, the loan amount, not including interest or income.

Real-Estate Broker: one who buys or sells property for another. A broker who has salespeople acting under his licensure is liable for their actions.

Rebate: a return of part of a payment.

Revolving Balance: a monetary amount on a credit card that accrues interest charges until it is paid in full.

Secured Debt: money owed that is attached to real or personal property.

Self-Proving Affidavit: a sworn statement by a testator and attesting witnesses before a notary public that a document is the testator's executed will. It allows the will to be probated during the life of the witnesses without their testimony.

Seller's Agent: a person who represents the seller's best interest in a real-estate transaction. This is not necessarily the same person as the listing agent.

Simple-Interest Loan: money borrowed in which the cost of borrowing accrues only on the original principal; as opposed to a *compound loan* whereby the cost of borrowing accrues on both the principal and interest.

Social Security: a federal program to benefit the retired, elderly, disabled and others in need, administered by the Social Security Administration.

Stock: a certificate that shows ownership of a specified number of shares in a company.

Stock Market: the business of exchanging stocks and other securities.

Subcontractor: a person who is hired to build, remodel or repair a structure.

Super-Discount Broker: a company that usually does not offer any services to its clients other than providing less expensive ways to purchase and sell investment products via the Internet or telephone. It may also be referred to as a deep-discount broker.

Tax-Assessed Value: the estimated worth of property, based on an appraisal, for county and city use.

Tax-Deferred Investment: money or capital placed in a fund whereby charges are paid at a later date, usually when the benefits are withdrawn.

Tax-Free Investment: money or capital placed in a fund whereby no charges are paid or owed when the benefits are withdrawn.

Term Life Insurance Policy: a written contract that provides coverage for a specified period, usually one year, and premium rates may increase as the policy is renewed as a result of the insured getting older and worldwide mortality rates. This type of policy accumulates no cash value.

Testator: one who makes and executes a will; term applies to males or general use. The word *testatrix* applies to females.

Time Share: the purchase of the use of property for a specified period.

Uninsured/Underinsured Motorist Protection: coverage against property damage and/or bodily injury if a person is involved in an automobile accident and the other person is at fault, but doesn't have liability coverage or doesn't have enough to cover the non-liable party's property damage and/or bodily injury.

Universal Life Insurance Policy: a written contract that provides permanent coverage as long as the premiums are paid. The premiums are invested in mutual funds, and thereby cash value may accumulate, but it is not guaranteed.

Unsecured Debt: money owed that is not attached to any real or personal property.

Whole Life Insurance Policy: a written contract that provides permanent coverage as long as the premiums are paid, which are higher for this type of policy because cash value is guaranteed. Cash value accumulates because dividends are paid by the insurance company based on the return of its investments.

Will: a person's (testator's) declaration of how he desires his property to be disposed of after his death; revocable during the lifetime of the testator, and is operable for no purpose until death.

Withholding Allowance: an amount of an employee's wages or salary that is deducted from his payroll income for tax purposes, based on the number of dependents/exemptions claimed.

INDEX

A

Adjusting to Changing Financial Circumstances, 167

Appliances/Furniture
buying, 58

Automobile
be prepared when shopping, 132
buying vs. leasing, 133-134
car notes, 131
"cheap" cars, 131
cloned versions, 133
comparing rental rates, 135
dealership repair/maintenance, 134
doing your own minor repairs, 134
driving for the heck of it, 136
emergency roadside assistance, 138
extended warranties, 132
parts, 134-135
pre-owned, 132-133
rental agreements, 136
tires, 135
traffic citations, 136-138
trading in, 132

Automobile Insurance. See *Insurance*

B

Banking
advertisements, 195
automated teller machines, 194
check-cashing fees, 194
direct deposit, 193
interest-bearing accounts, 195
monthly fees, 194-195

Bankruptcy
Chapter Seven, 33-35
Chapter Thirteen, 33-35

Beauty
body piercings/tattoos, 116
cosmetics, 115
cosmetic surgery, 115-116
doing your own hair, 115
doing your own nails, 115, 116

Becoming Low-Maintenance, 172

Becoming Organized, 41

Billing Statements, 172

Borrowing Money, 165

Budgeting
establishing, 37-38
making it rewarding, 38

Building Your Own House, 83-88

Buying the Display, 58

C

Car. See *Automobile*

Career
continuing-education credits, 129
getting your company to fund your education, 128
raises, 129
résumés, 129
starting a home-based business, 129-130
value of an education, 127
when to look for another job, 128-129

Caring for Your Belongings, 163

Children
activity costs, 155
as students, 154-155
buying clothes/shoes, 153
buying into fads, 154
child-care costs, 151-152
private vs. public schools, 152
saving for college, 154-155
saying no, 153
teaching budgeting, 153
teaching money management, 153
throwing parties, 154

LET'S GET READY FOR A SECOND EDITION

Please take a few minutes to answer the following questions.
We'd love to hear from you!

Has this book been helpful to you? If so, how?

If not, what would make it more helpful?

What are some things you would like to see added?

Do you have a money-saving suggestion you would like to share with others?

Send your comments to:

Brown Bag Press
P.O. Box 764585
Dallas, Texas 75376

Or, visit our Web site at: **www.brownbagpress.com**

Thank you for your time.

BORROWED THIS BOOK?
WANT A COPY OF YOUR OWN?
KNOW SOMEONE WHO NEEDS A COPY?

Quick Mail-Order Form

Please print the following information:

Name _____

Address _____

City _____ State _____ Zip _____

Telephone _____ E-mail _____

_____ books @ **$14.95** each = $ _____

Shipping & Handling $ _____
($3 first book, $2 each additional copy)

Sales Tax $ _____
(Texas residents add 8.25%)

Total Amount Enclosed $ _____

Make check or money order payable to:
Brown Bag Press
P.O. Box 764585
Dallas, Texas 75376

Or, log on to **www.brownbagpress.com**
to confirm up-to-date ordering information.